Joanna Forbes L'Estrange
A Season to Sing

A choral re-imagining of Vivaldi's *The Four Seasons*

Vocal Score

RSCM PUBLICATIONS is the trading name of RSCM Enterprises Ltd,
a wholly owned subsidiary of
THE ROYAL SCHOOL OF CHURCH MUSIC
19 The Close, Salisbury, SP1 2EB, England
Registered charity 312828

Tel: +44 (0)1722 424848
E-mail: press@rscm.com Website: www.rscmshop.com

Joanna Forbes L'Estrange
A Season to Sing

A choral re-imagining of Vivaldi's *The Four Seasons*

*Joanna Forbes L'Estrange has asserted her moral rights
to be identified as the composer of this work.*

All rights reserved. No part of this publication may be reproduced, stored in a retrieval system, or transmitted, in any form or by any means, without the prior permission in writing of the copyright holders, or as expressly permitted by law.

Permission to perform this work in public or to make a recording of this work should normally be obtained from PRS for Music at www.prsformusic.com or its affiliated Societies in each country throughout the world, unless the owner or the occupier of the premises being used holds a licence from the Society.

RSCM Catalogue Number RS63

ISBN: 978-0-85402-351-6

Cover design: Anthony Marks
Front cover image: Marco Ricci (Belluno 1676-Venice 1730)
Landscape with Cattle and a Woman Speaking to a Seated Man
Royal Collection Trust Picture Library
Music Engraving: Donald Thomson
Organ part realisation: Alexander L'Estrange
Printed in Great Britain by Short Run Press Ltd, Exeter

For Arndy, with love

To every thing there is a season
And a time to every purpose under Heaven

Ecclesiastes 3:1

Foreword

Re-imagining an instrumental work for voices has precedence, of course. Some thirty years after composing *Adagio for Strings* Samuel Barber added the words of the *Agnus Dei* to his music, creating from the original strings piece an entirely new one for choir. Perhaps more common is for an adaptation to be made by someone other than the composer of the original work, for instance with the pop song *All By Myself* which is based on the slow movement of Rachmaninoff's *Piano Concerto No.2 in C minor*. So too with the hymn *I vow to thee, my country* which started life as a wordless melody within the Jupiter movement of *The Planets* by Holst. *Jazz Sébastien Bach*, the debut album by the 1960s Swingle Singers, comprised instrumental music by J.S. Bach ingeniously arranged by Ward Swingle for eight jazz-scatting vocalists with double bass and drums.

In all of these examples, the re-imagining in no way diminishes our respect for the original composition. On the contrary it offers a new perspective, for performer and listener alike, akin to a novel being turned into a play or film. So it was that I found myself pondering how Vivaldi's four violin concertos, published in 1725 as *The Four Seasons*, might fare as choral pieces. Having loved this music since I was young girl, I'd often had the thought that melodies as good as these deserve to be sung. With 2025 marking the 300th anniversary of this most famous of the so-called Red Priest's compositions, it seemed the perfect time to put pencil to manuscript paper and give it a go. Nine months later, *A Season to Sing* was born.

Sourcing the poems, hymn texts and Bible passages for each movement was an integral part of the process. It mattered to me that the words might sound as if they could have inspired the music, even though it was the other way round. This meant matching their rhythms, rhyme schemes, phrase lengths and cadences to Vivaldi's melodies whilst simultaneously enhancing the all-important programmatic depictions within the different seasons. Vivaldi's manuscript helpfully contains the Italian sonnets he wrote as the basis for his music. For the opening movement of Winter, I chose to adapt one of these sonnets, *L'Inverno*, to create a soundscape. This is followed by the only wordless movement of the piece which I arranged in homage to Ward Swingle, the founder of The Swingle Singers, who became a close friend during my tenure as the group's Musical Director. The remaining texts are from the Old Testament (Genesis, Exodus, Psalms, Song of Solomon and Zechariah), poems by two 19th-century English poets Emily Brontë and Eliza Cook, a hymn by Henry Alford and a Thomas Morley madrigal. It's an eclectic mix into which I added the words of Ecclesiastes 3:1–8 (beginning 'To every thing there is a season') and set them in two movements which serve as bookends to the twelve Vivaldi movements. My settings were written in a quasi-Baroque style with its pleasing circles of 5ths and melodic sequences.

As a performer of contemporary and avant-garde music, I relish opportunities to create sounds in ways beyond conventional singing. *A Season to Sing* contains many such passages for the choir, including a whistling bird chorus, the evocation of a storm with the use of body percussion, a bagpipe's drone and the call of the cuckoo, as well as half-whispered, staccato syllables and jaw-wobble shivers to portray a freezing cold winter. It is my hope that choirs of all kinds will have plenty of fun when rehearsing and performing this work and that audiences will enjoy hearing familiar music presented in a new way.

It was important to me from the outset that *A Season to Sing* be performable by upper voice choirs as well as by mixed voice choirs. Vivaldi famously spent much of his working life providing a first-class musical education to orphaned girls at the Ospedale della Pietà in Venice, teaching them everything from playing instruments and singing to copying and composing their own music. Whereas boys were apprenticed out from the age of 10 to learn a trade, girls remained at the orphanage and those who were selected for musical training formed instrumental ensembles and choirs. Their all-female concerts were a major tourist attraction in Venice at the time, drawing the attention of royalty and nobility, and many of his pupils went on to become professional musicians. Vivaldi composed his *Gloria* for the Pietà choir and it is widely believed that it was his pupil Anna Maria della Pietà, an exceptional violinist, who inspired him to compose *The Four Seasons*. Knowing that Vivaldi was a fellow champion of female musicians makes me respect him all the more.

I am indebted to the fifty-five choirs around the world who co-commissioned *A Season to Sing*, several of which are upper voice choirs, and grateful to the Royal School of Church Music for inviting me to compose this my first full-scale choral work. Finally, I offer a deep bow to Antonio Vivaldi whose extraordinary music, which sounds as fresh today as it must have done 300 years ago, captured my imagination and inspired me to compose this piece.

Joanna Forbes L'Estrange
October 2024

Joanna Forbes L'Estrange in Vivaldi's church, Venice, April 2024

Contents

1.	A Time to Dance	1

SPRING

2.	Welcome Spring	5
3.	Music, Sweet Music	17
4.	To the Bagpipe's Sound	29

SUMMER

5.	Sing Cuccu!	35
6.	Trees Lending Shelter	42
7.	Summer Storm	44

AUTUMN

8.	Song of Harvest	51
9.	Falling Autumn Leaves	60
10.	Make a Joyful Noise	65

WINTER

11.	Winter Freeze	72
12.	Cosy Indoors (while outside it pours)	83
13.	While Earth Remaineth	91
14.	A Time of Peace	102

Performance notes	109
List of commissioning choirs	112
More choral pieces by Joanna Forbes L'Estrange	114

1. A Time to Dance

Ecclesiastes 3:1–4 (KJV)

Joanna Forbes L'Estrange

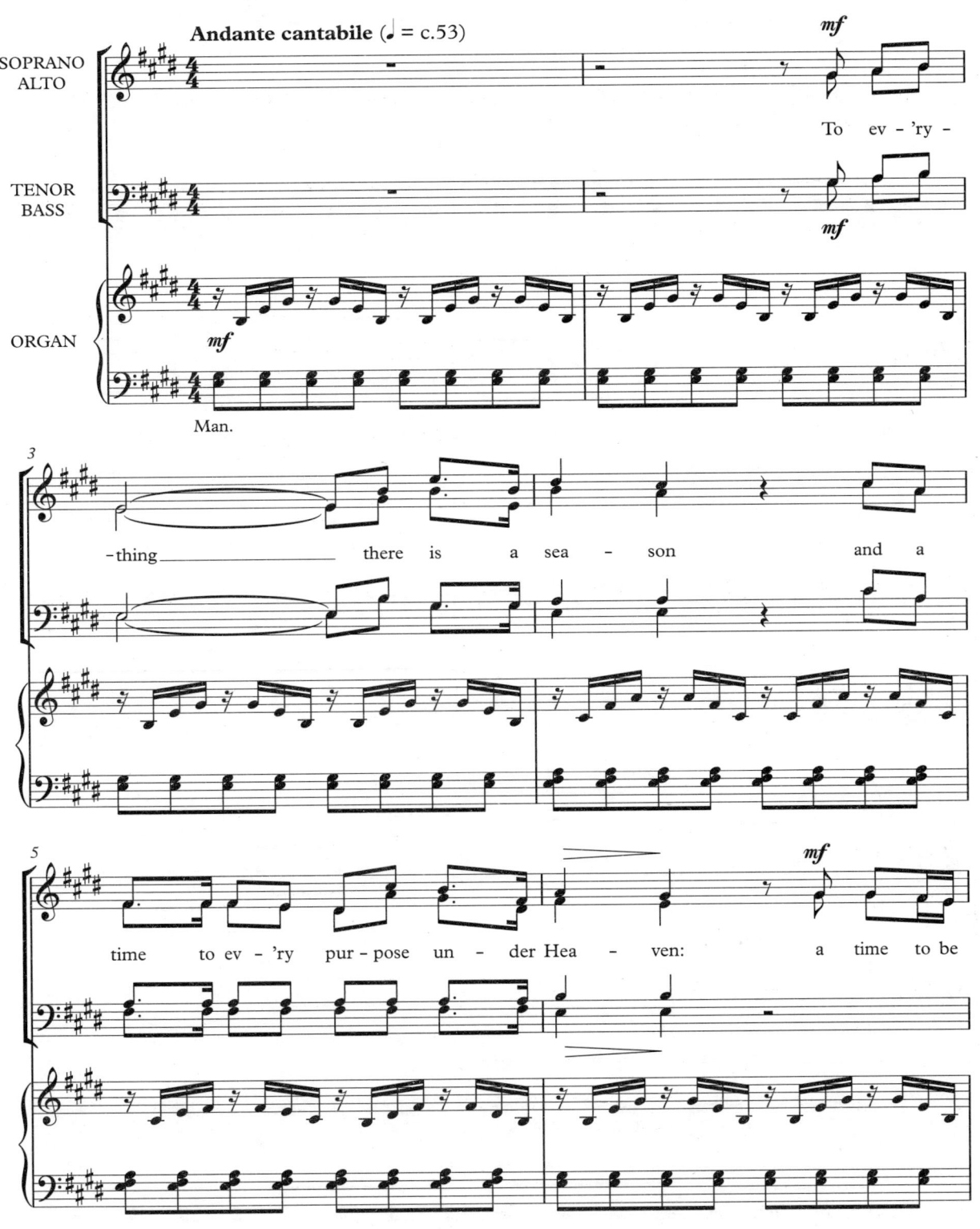

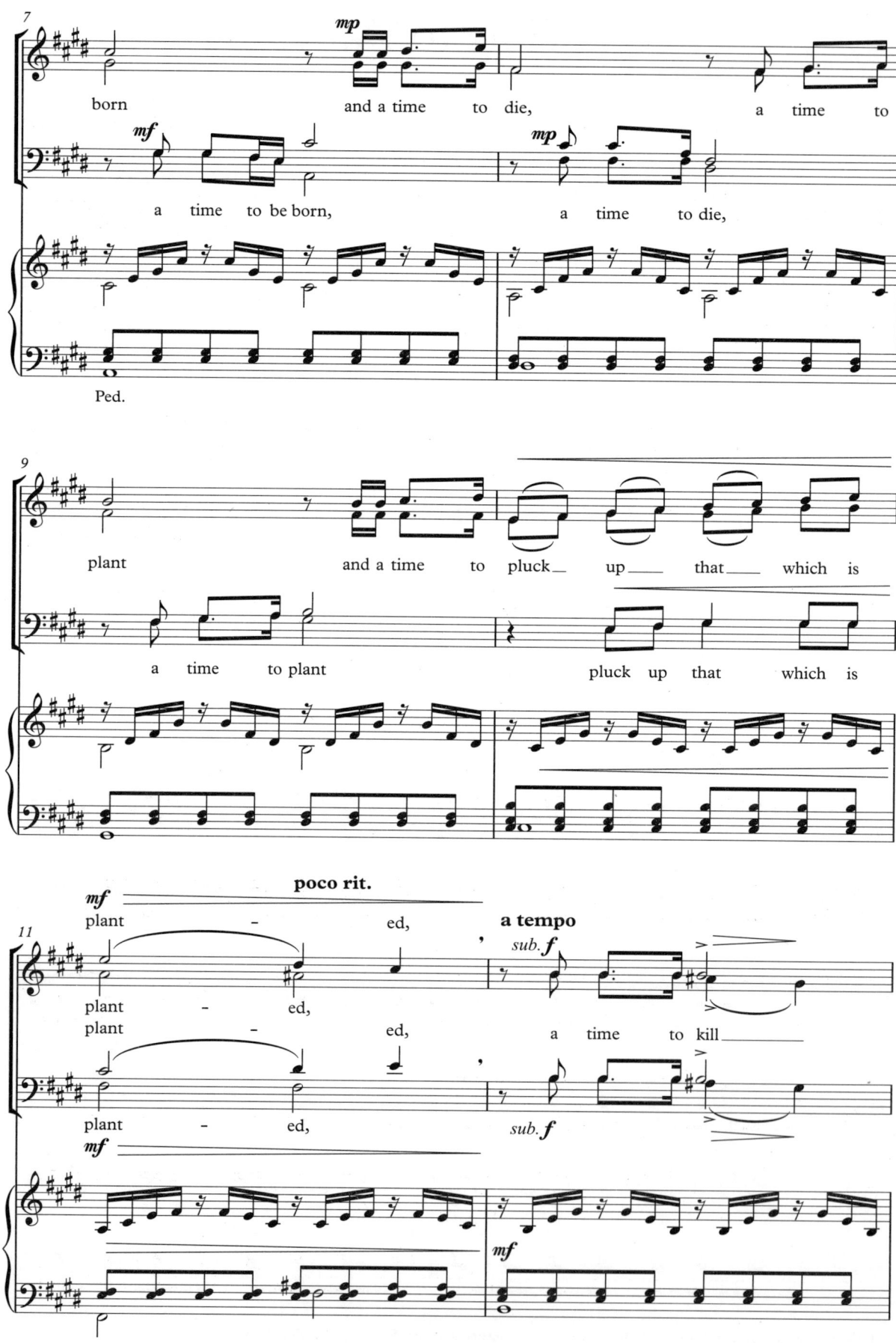

SPRING

2. Welcome Spring

Thomas Morley madrigal 'Now is the month of Maying', based on Orazio Vecchi
Joanna Forbes L'Estrange, based on Zechariah 10:1 (NIV) and Song of Solomon 2:11–13 (KJV)

Antonio Vivaldi arr. Joanna Forbes L'Estrange

11
spring - ing and now the birds are sing - ing, they're sing - ing to
earth and now the birds are sing - ing to

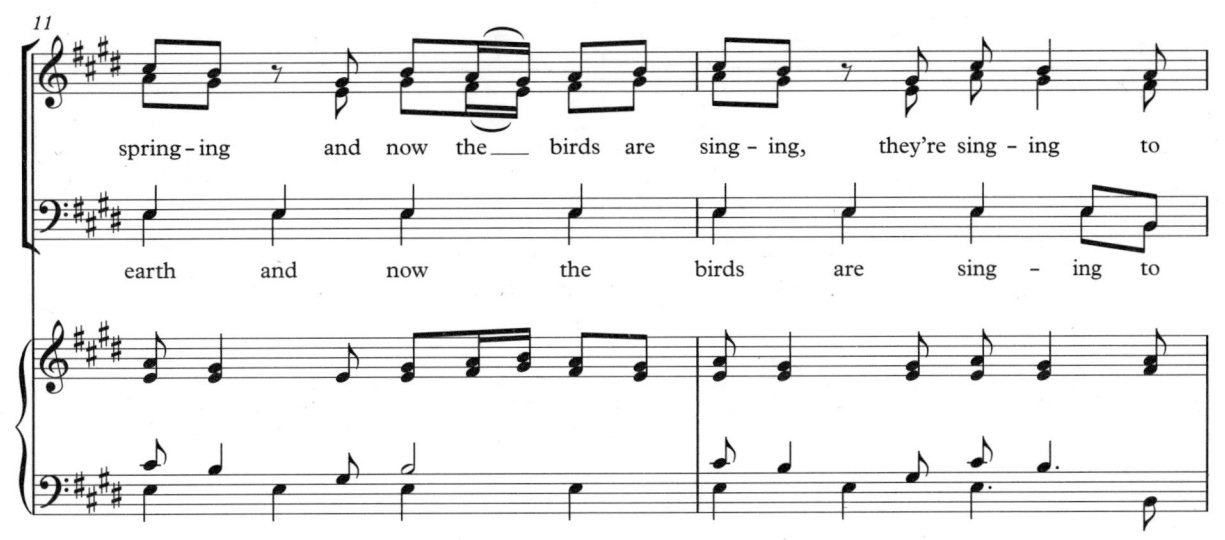

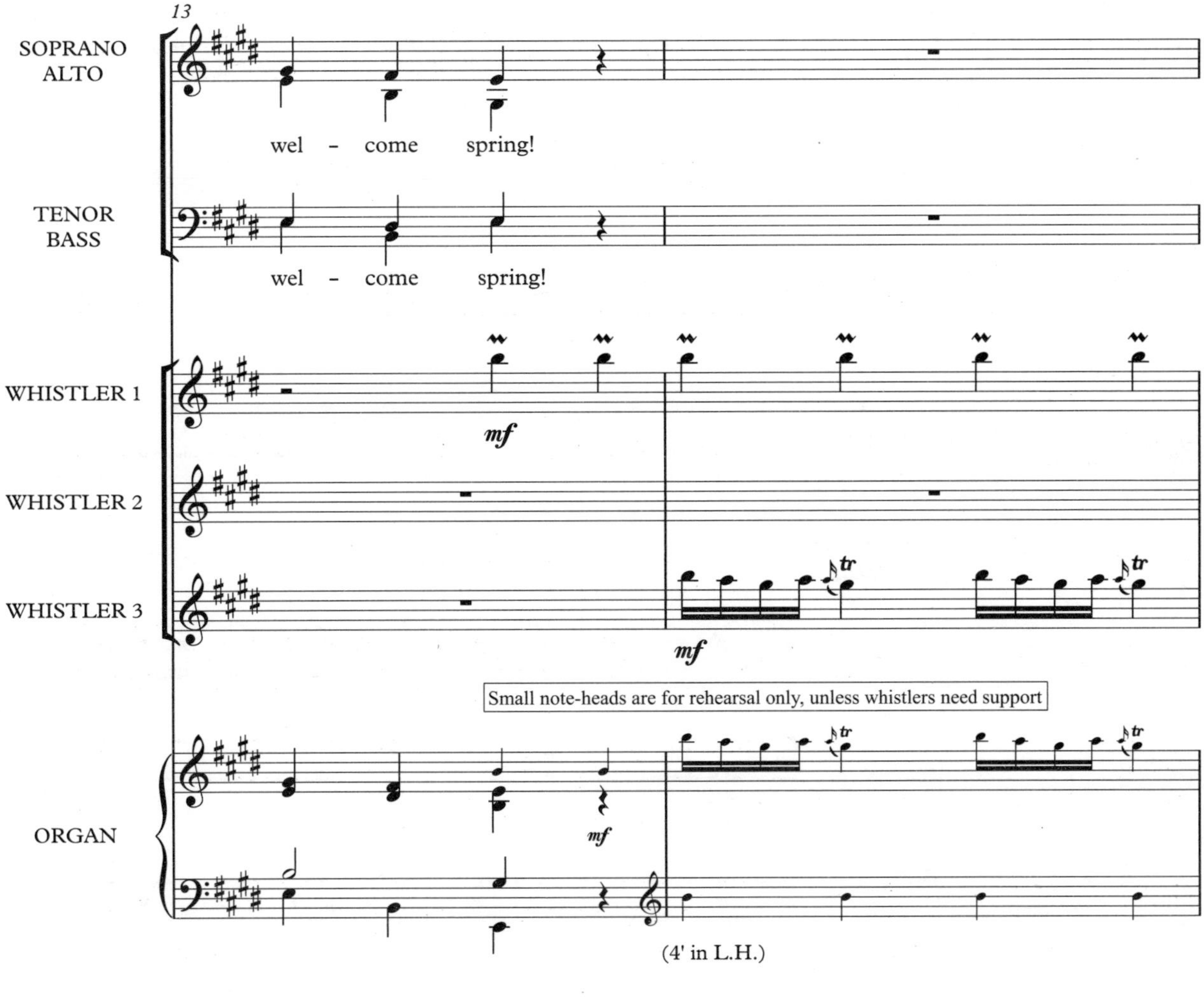
13
SOPRANO
ALTO
wel - come spring!
TENOR
BASS
wel - come spring!
WHISTLER 1
mf
WHISTLER 2
WHISTLER 3
tr
mf
Small note-heads are for rehearsal only, unless whistlers need support
ORGAN
mf
(4' in L.H.)

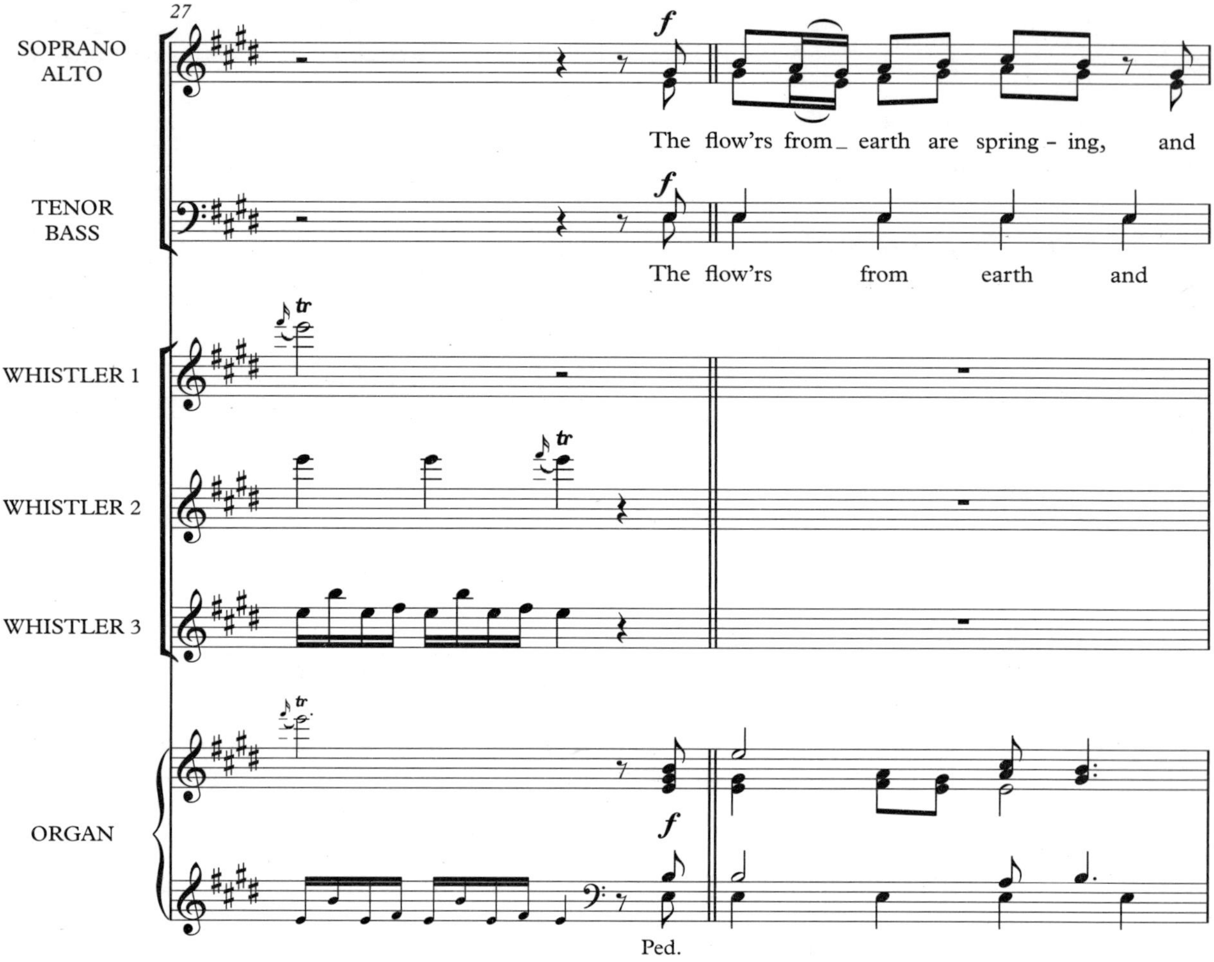
27
SOPRANO
ALTO
f
The flow'rs from _ earth are spring - ing, and
TENOR
BASS
f
The flow'rs from earth and
WHISTLER 1
tr
WHISTLER 2
tr
WHISTLER 3
tr
ORGAN
f
Ped.

29
mp
now the _ birds are sing - ing, they're sing - ing to wel - come spring! We wel -
We wel -
mp
now the birds are sing - ing to wel - come spring! We wel - come
mp

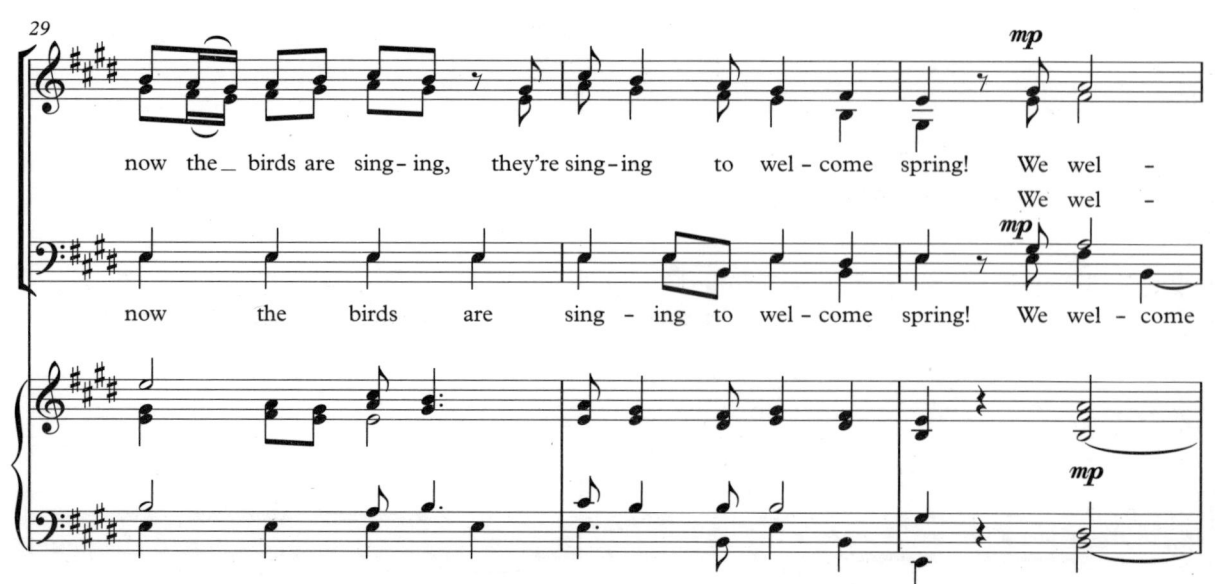

3. Music, Sweet Music

Eliza Cook poem 'Spring' vv.2 & 3

Antonio Vivaldi arr.
Joanna Forbes L'Estrange

19
birth.
Man.

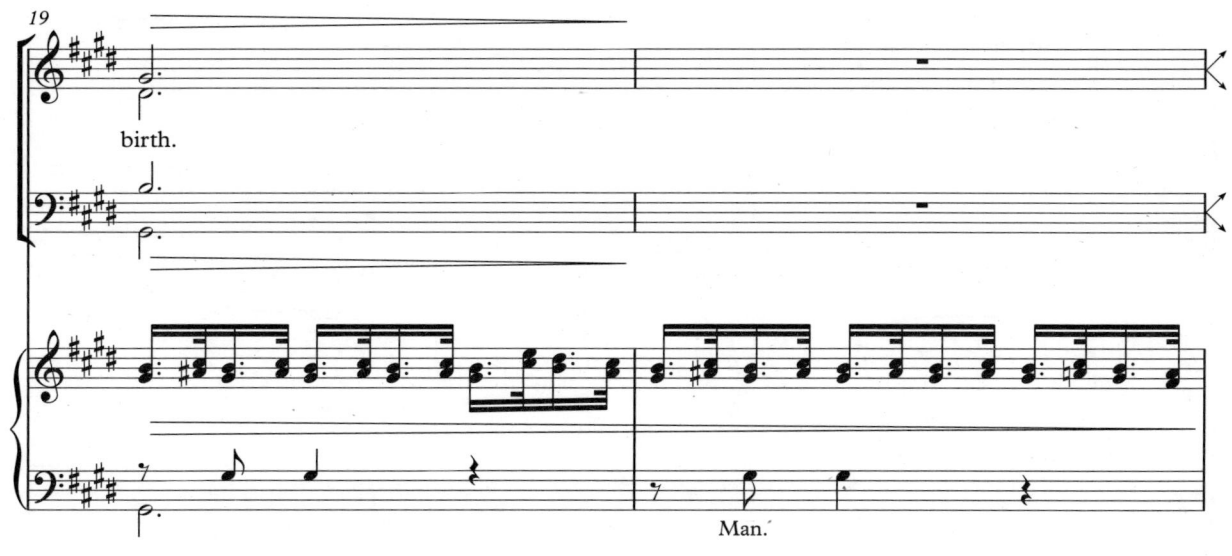

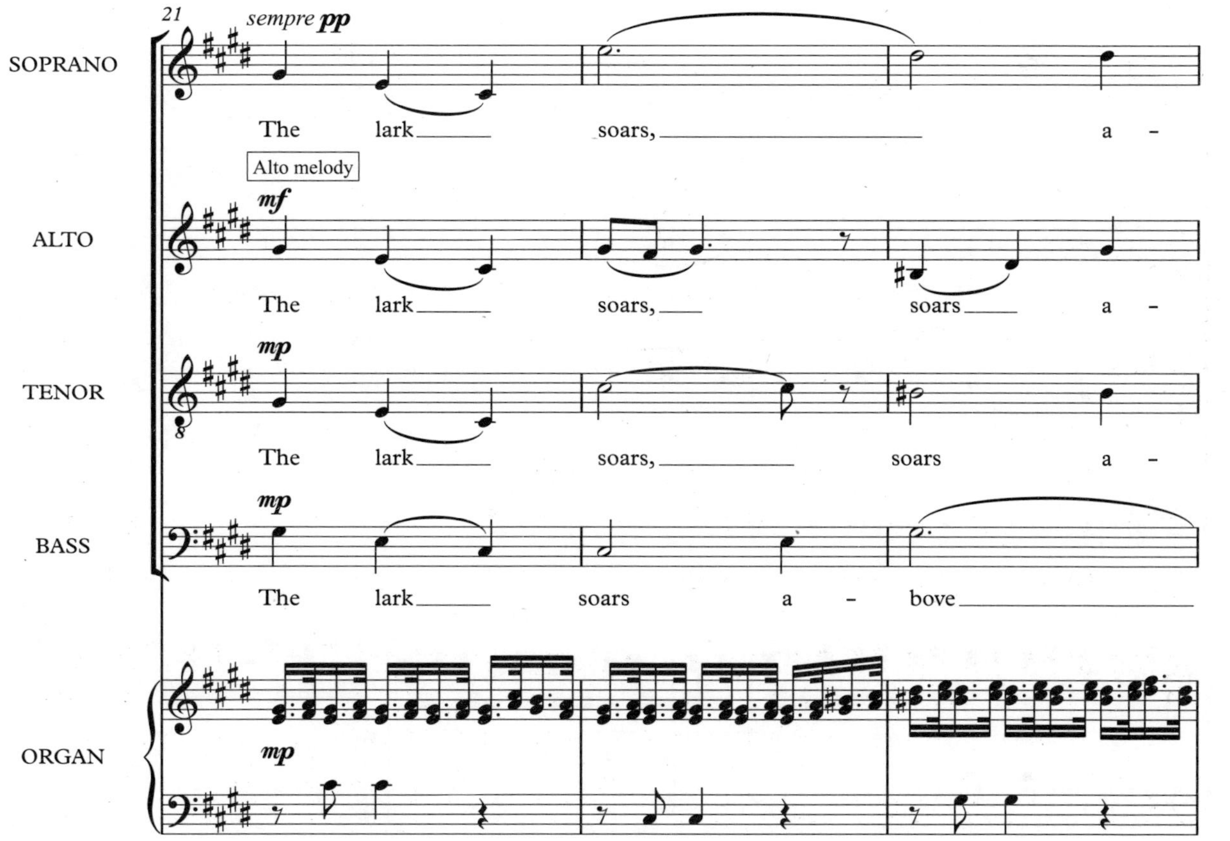
21
sempre pp
SOPRANO
The lark soars, a –
Alto melody
mf
ALTO
The lark soars, soars a –
mp
TENOR
The lark soars, soars a –
mp
BASS
The lark soars a – bove
ORGAN
mp

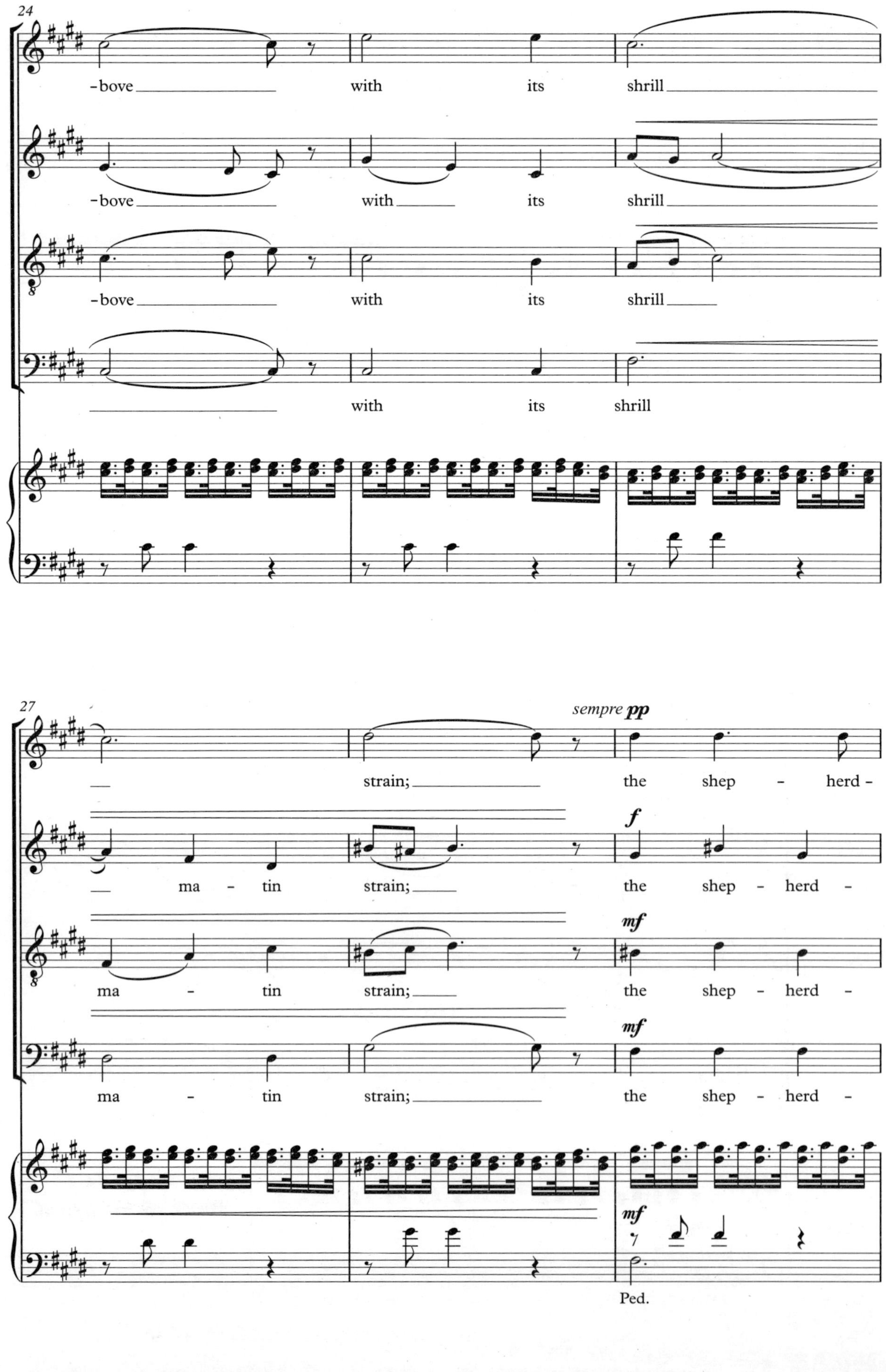
24
-bove with its shrill
-bove with its shrill
-bove with its shrill
with its shrill
27
sempre pp
strain; the shep - herd -
f
ma - tin strain; the shep - herd -
mf
ma - tin strain; the shep - herd -
mf
ma - tin strain; the shep - herd -
mf
Ped.

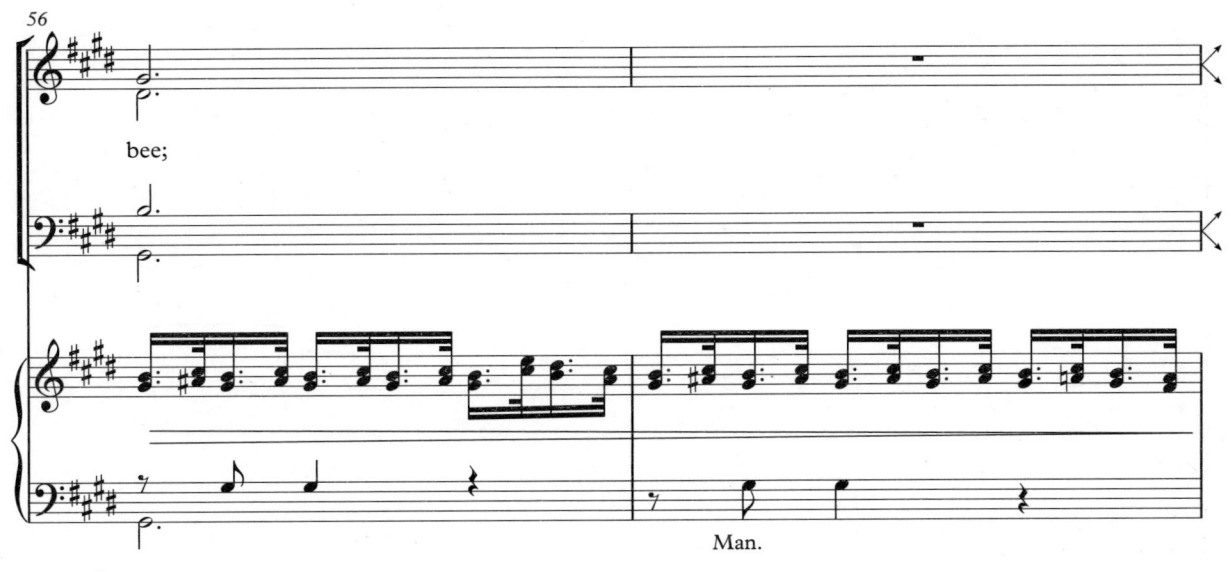

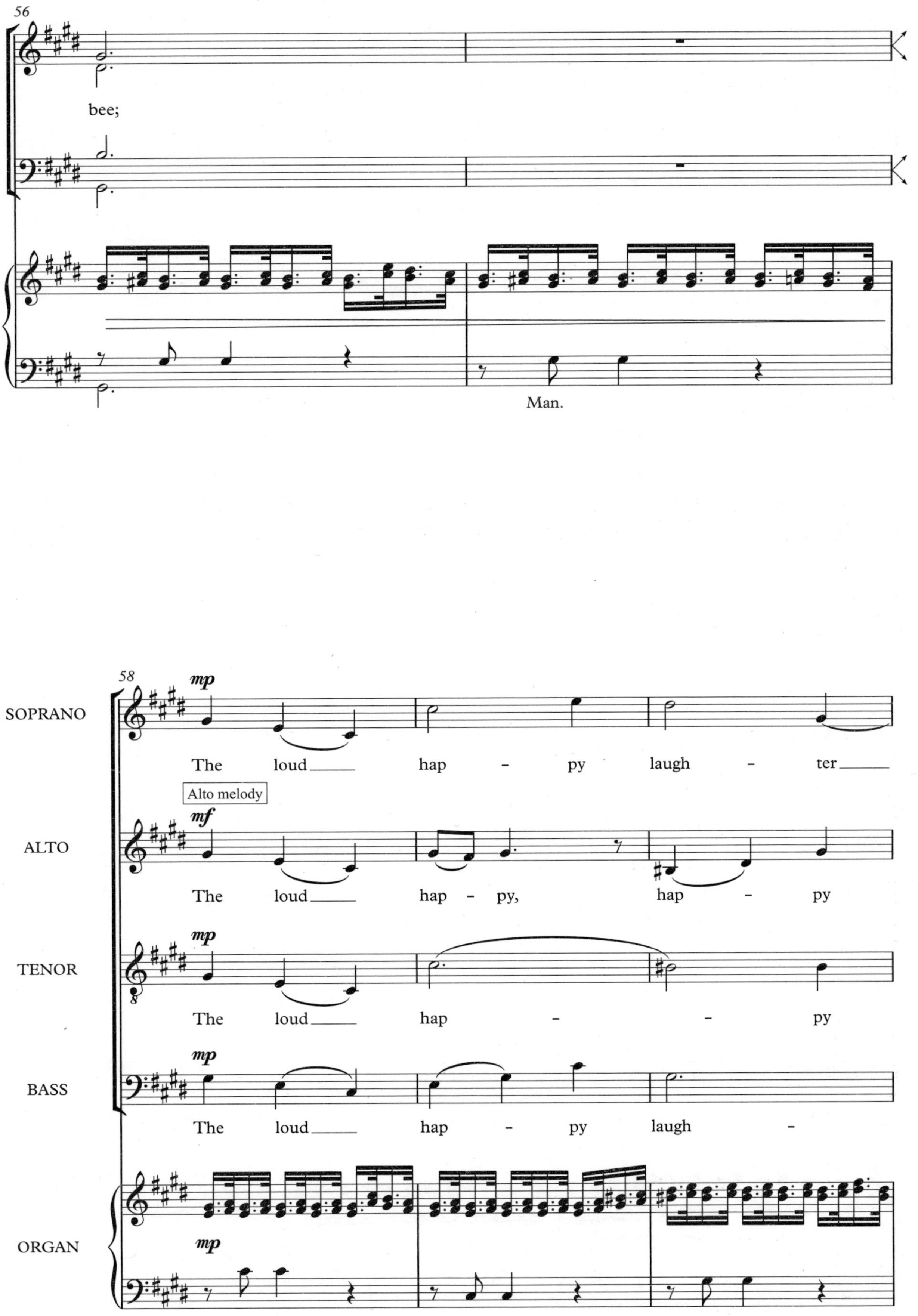
56
bee;
Man.
58
SOPRANO
mp
The loud hap - py laugh - ter
Alto melody
ALTO
mf
The loud hap - py, hap - py
TENOR
mp
The loud hap - - py
BASS
mp
The loud hap - py laugh -
ORGAN
mp

4. To the Bagpipe's Sound

Thomas Morley madrigal 'Now is the month of Maying', based on Orazio Vecchi

Antonio Vivaldi arr. Joanna Forbes L'Estrange

*as nasal as possible, to mimic a bagpipe's drone

SUMMER

5. Sing Cuccu!

Emily Brontë poem 'Moonlight, Summer Moonlight' v.1
Anon. 'Sumer is icumen in'
Additional words by Joanna Forbes L'Estrange

Antonio Vivaldi arr.
Joanna Forbes L'Estrange

* Each time the word 'soft' occurs, the singers are encouraged to create a special effect by moving onto the unvoiced 'f' consonant sooner than is customary.

* Pronounced *Lhu* (as in 'loo')

* Pronounced *thu* (as in 'thoo')

* Pronounced *ne* (as in '<u>ne</u>ver') *swik* (as it looks) *thu* (as in 'th<u>oo</u>') *naver* (as it looks) *nu* (as in 'noo')

6. Trees Lending Shelter

Emily Brontë poem 'Moonlight, Summer Moonlight' vv.1 & 2

Antonio Vivaldi arr.
Joanna Forbes L'Estrange

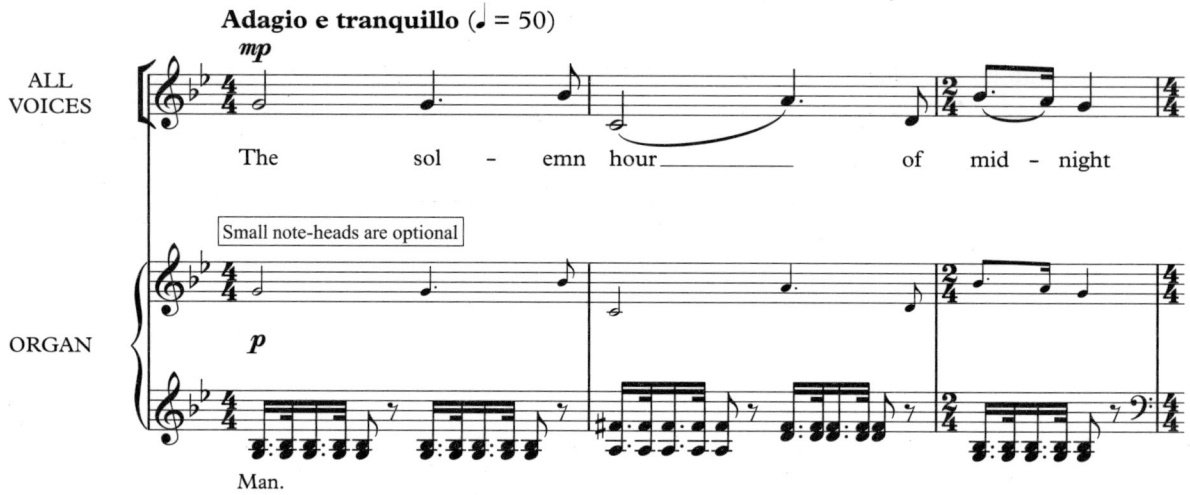

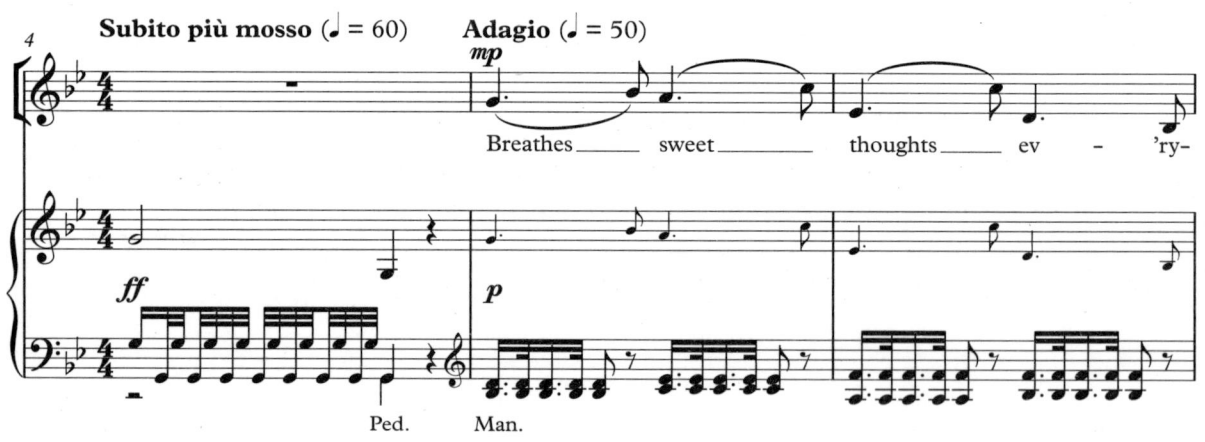

*After the final chord, the choir places vocal scores on chairs, music stands or floor, open or with a marker at page 46.

7. Summer Storm

Psalm 77:17–18 (NKJV)

Antonio Vivaldi arr.
Joanna Forbes L'Estrange

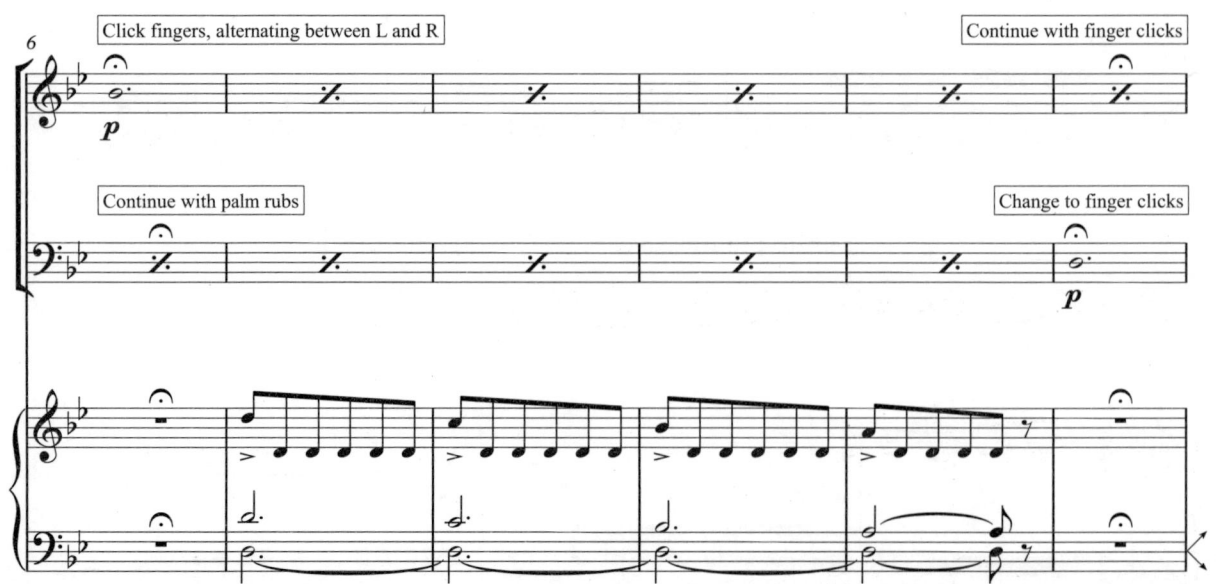

* Note the voice pairings.
  Storm soundscape is created by layering body percussion, each singer at their own pace. Conductor cues each effect.

46

* or, if possible, jump with both feet landing on the downbeat!

AUTUMN

8. Song of Harvest

Henry Alford hymn 'Come, Ye Thankful People, Come' v.1
Exodus 34:21 (KJV)

Antonio Vivaldi arr.
Joanna Forbes L'Estrange

32
- venth day you shall rest,
har-vest sea-son, e-ven dur-ing plough-ing sea-son, e-ven dur-ing har - vest,
har-vest sea-son, en dur-ing plough-ing sea-son, e-ven dur-ing har - vest,

35
On the se - venth day you
E-ven dur-ing plough-ing sea-son, e-ven dur-ing har-vest sea-son, e-ven dur-ing plough-ing sea-son,
Ev-en dur-ing plough-ing sea-son, ev-en dur-ing har-vest sea-son, ev-en dur-ing plough-ing sea-son,
V.S.

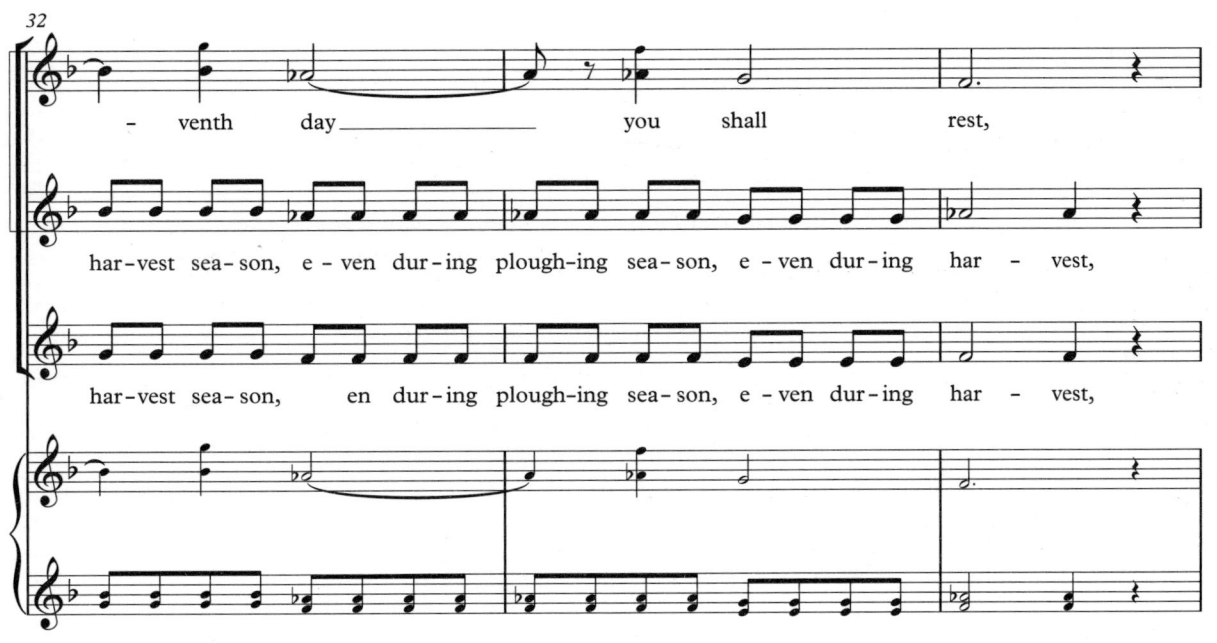

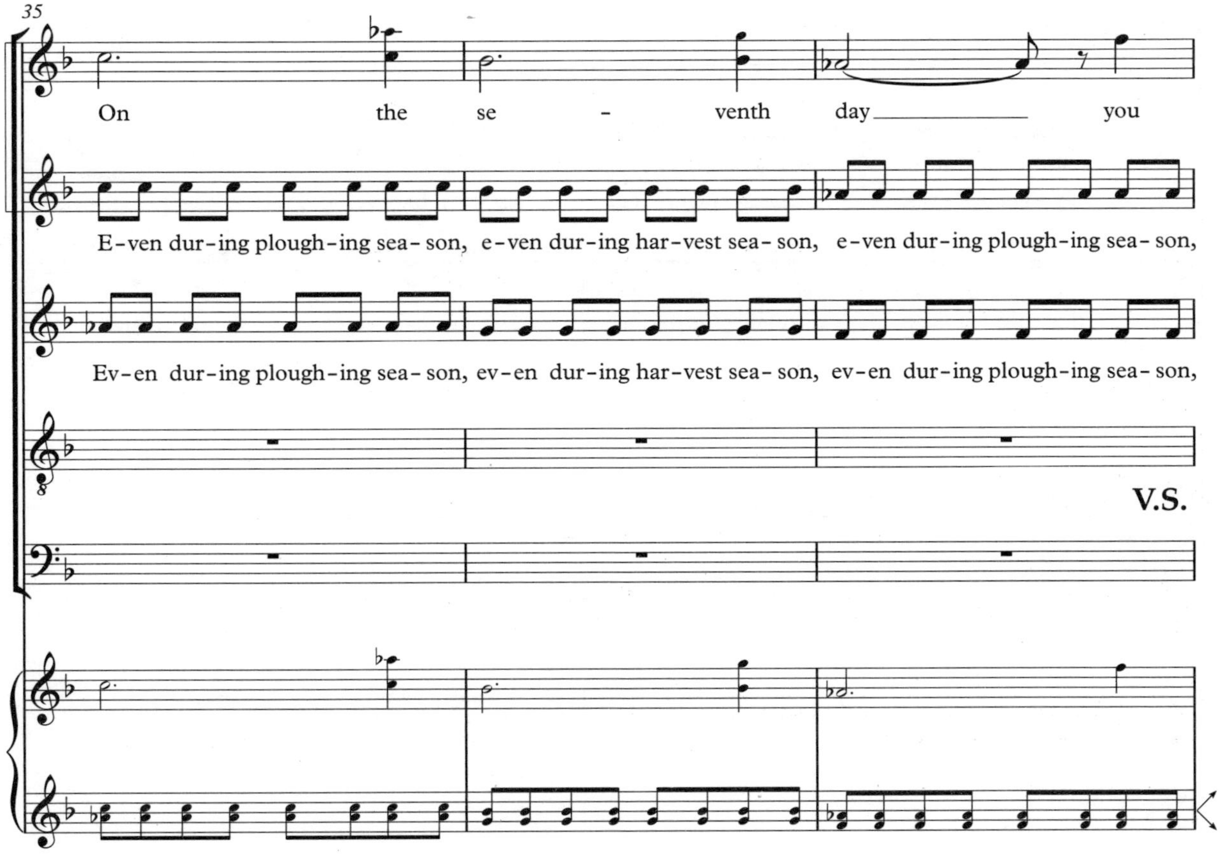

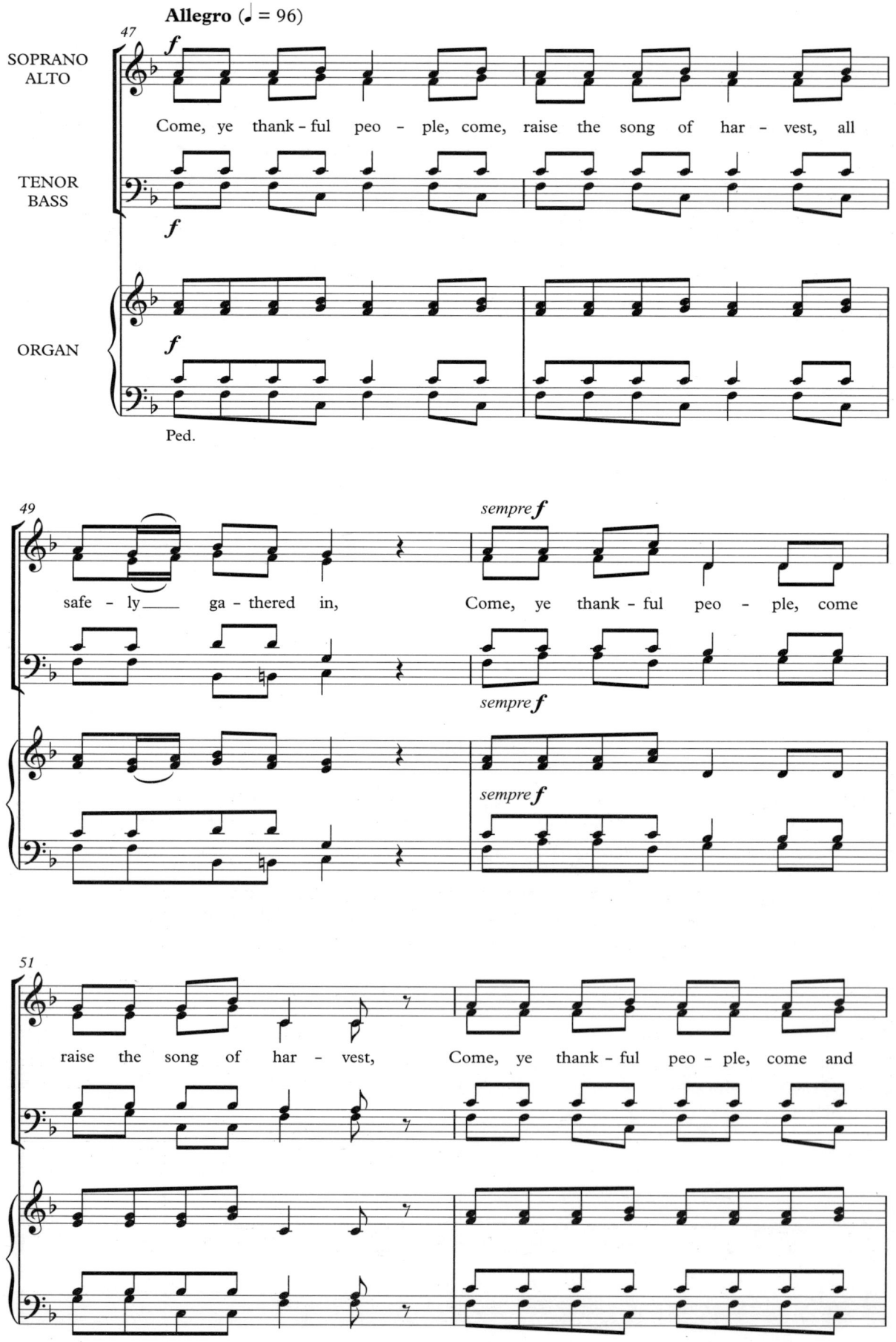

9. Falling Autumn Leaves

Emily Brontë poem 'Fall, Leaves, Fall' lines 1–4

Antonio Vivaldi arr.
Joanna Forbes L'Estrange

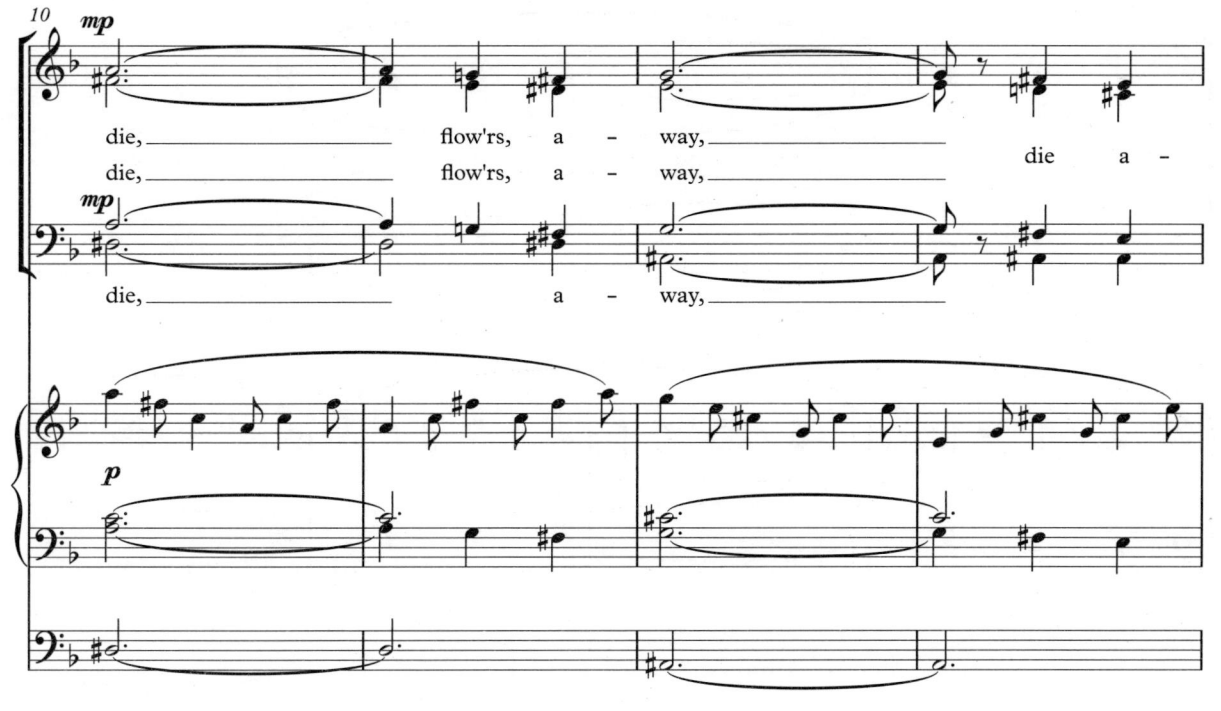

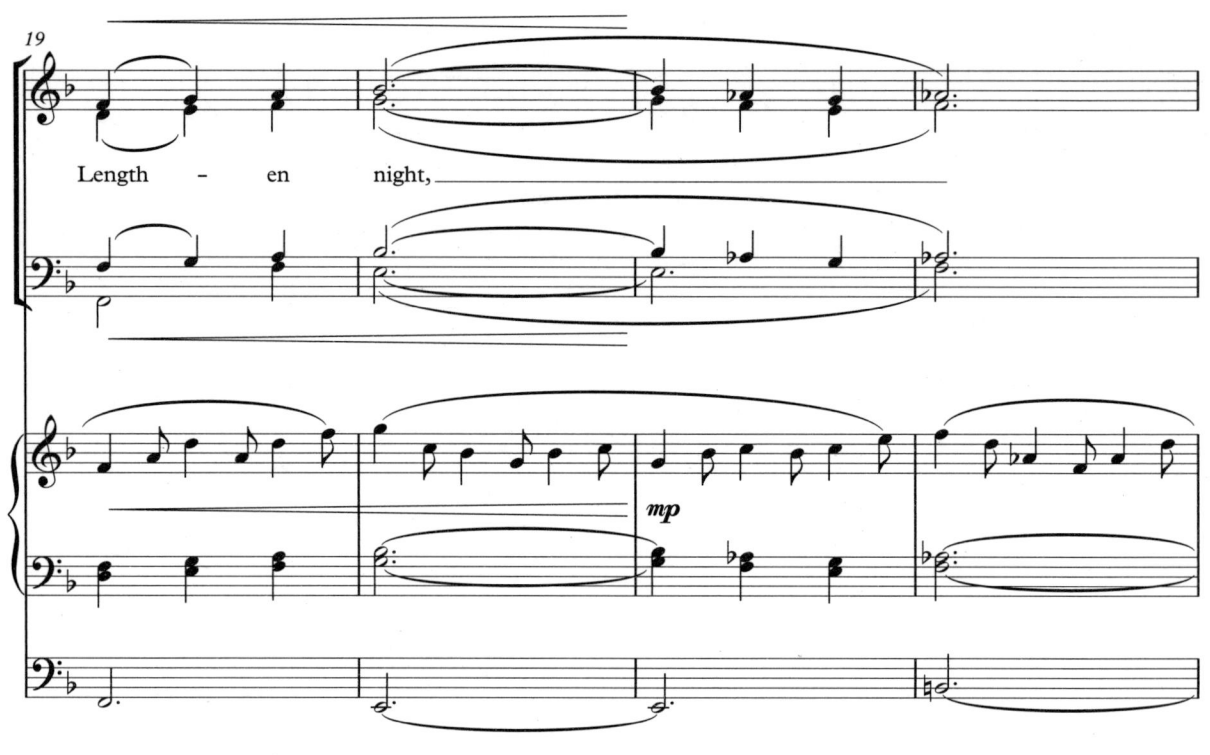
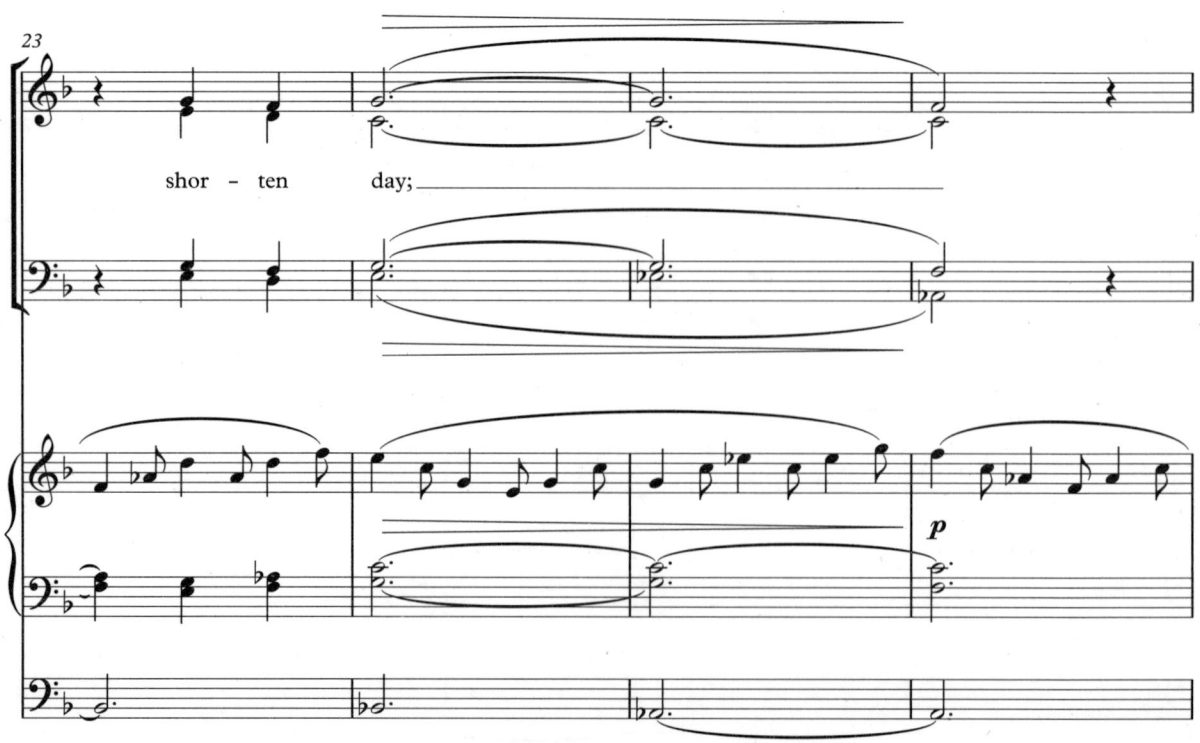

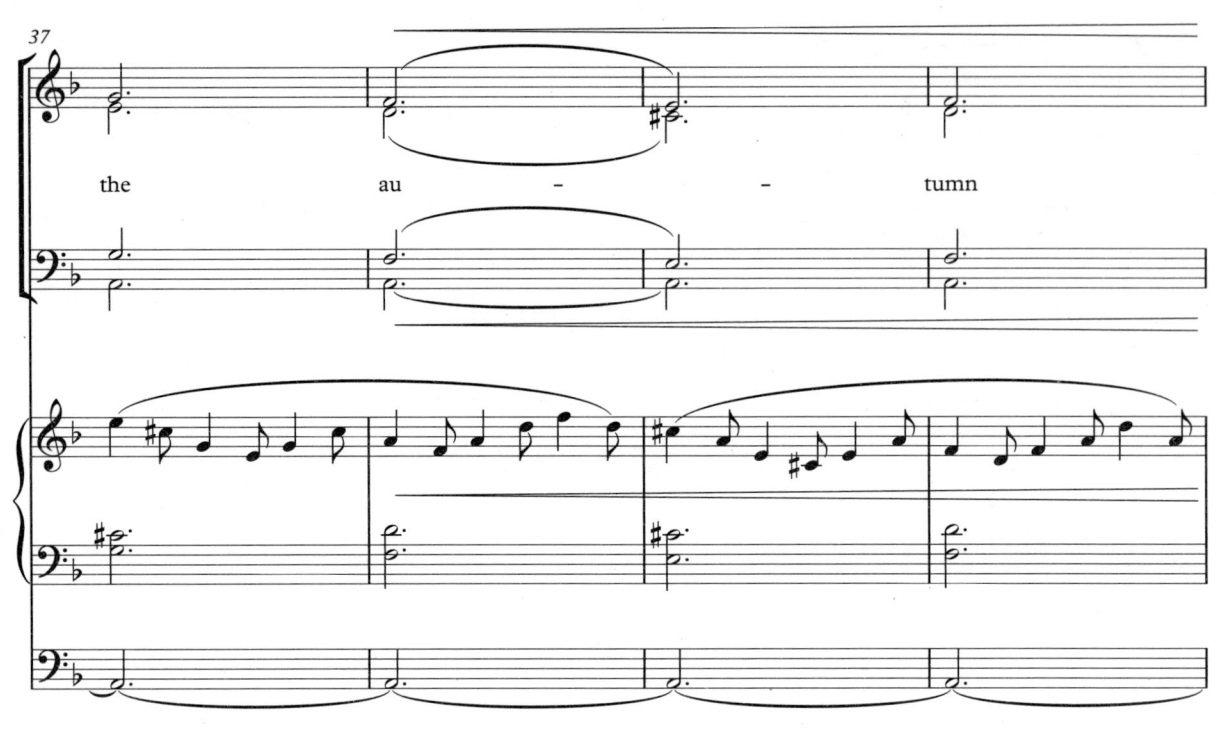
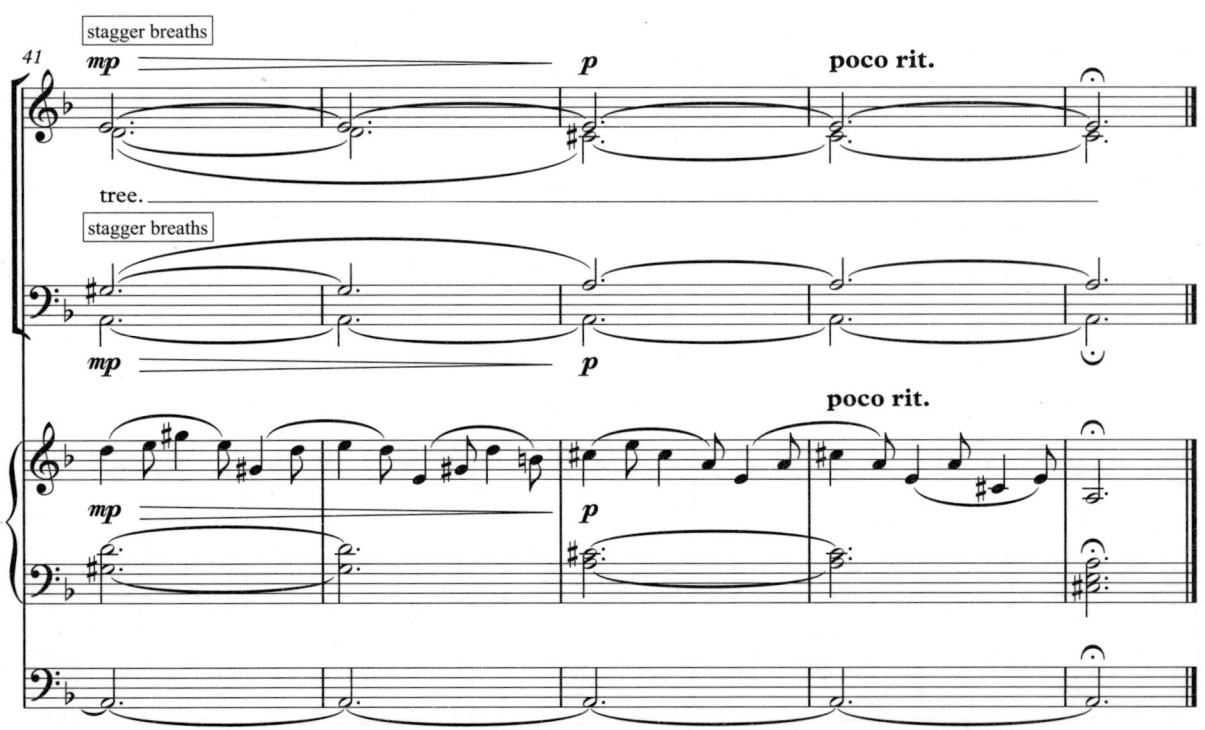

10. Make a Joyful Noise

Psalm 100:1–2 (KJV)
Psalm 150:3–6 (KJV)

Antonio Vivaldi arr.
Joanna Forbes L'Estrange

WINTER

11. Winter Freeze

Antonio Vivaldi sonnet 'L'Inverno'
(see performance notes for translation)

Antonio Vivaldi arr.
Joanna Forbes L'Estrange

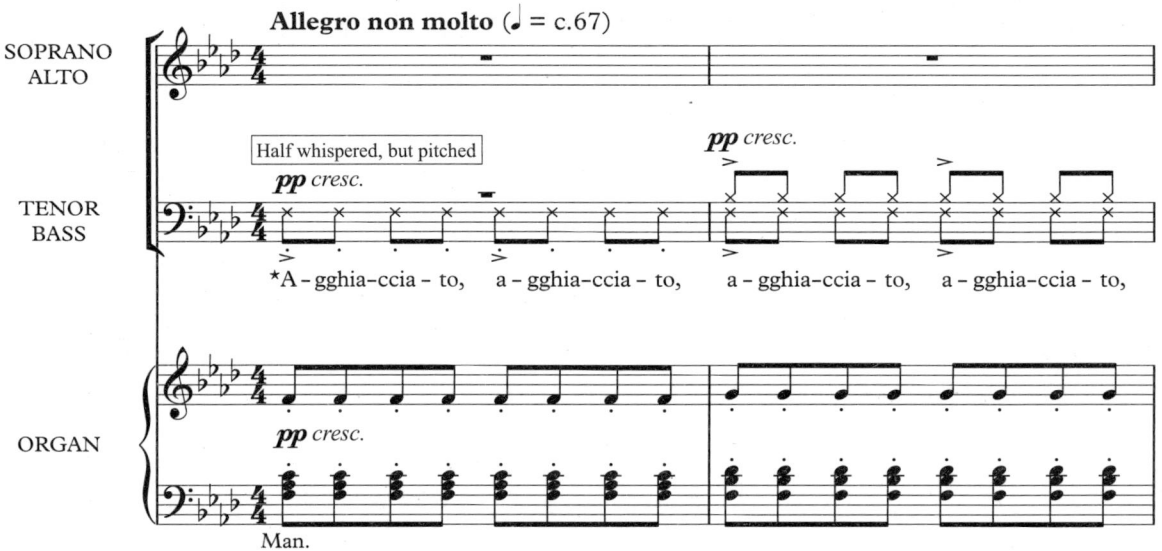

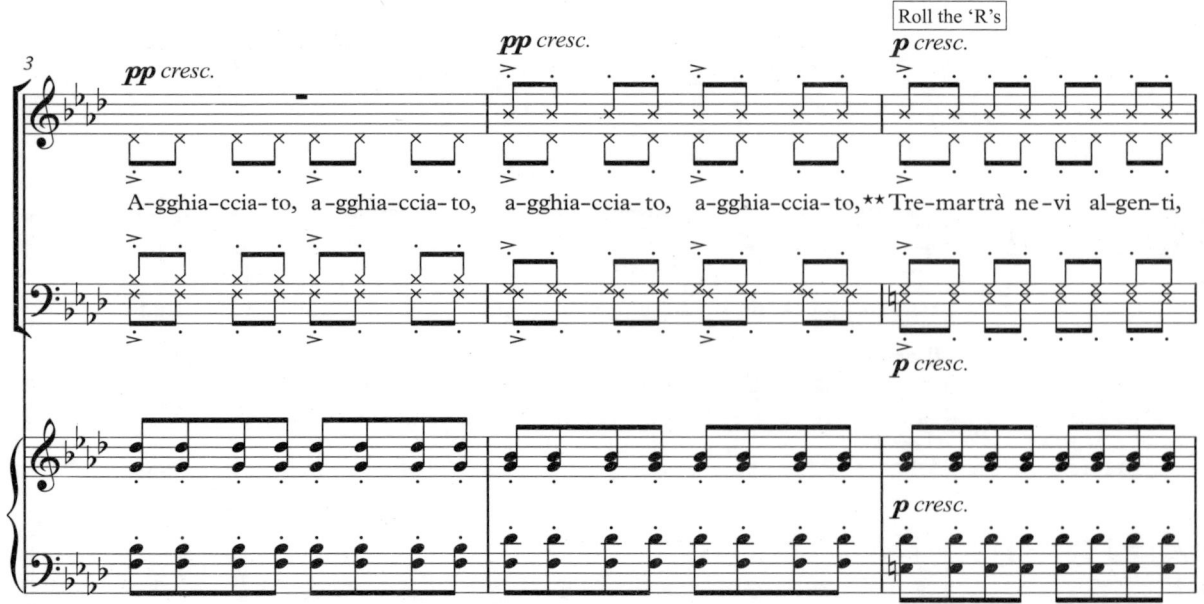

* Pronounced *a* (as in '<u>a</u>m') *gghia* ('gee-a' as one syllable: 'g-ya') *ccia* (as in '<u>ch</u>aff') *to* (as in '<u>do</u>t')

** Pronounced *tre* (as in '<u>tre</u>ad') *mar* (as in '<u>mar</u>ch') *trà* (as in '<u>tra</u>d') *ne* (as in '<u>ne</u>ver') *vi* (as in '<u>ve</u>al')
al (as in '<u>al</u>paca') *gen* (as in '<u>gen</u>tle') *ti* (as in '<u>dea</u>l')

* Pronounced *Al* (as in '<u>Al</u>istair') *Se* (as in '<u>se</u>ven') *ve* (as in '<u>ve</u>ry') *ro* (as in '<u>ro</u>bin')
** Pronounced *Spi* (as in '<u>spi</u>rit') *i* (as in '<u>i</u>t') *ra* (as in '<u>ra</u>bbit') *d'o* (as in '<u>do</u>t') *rri* (as in '<u>re</u>ach') *do* (as in '<u>do</u>t') *ven* (as in '<u>ven</u>t') *to* (as in '<u>do</u>t')

* Pronounced *cor* (as in 'gone') *rer* (as in 'rare') *bat* (as in 'bat') *ten* (as in 'dent') *do* (as in 'dot')
** Pronounced *i* (as in 'eat') *pie* ('pyay') *di* (as in 'deal') *og* (as in 'on') *ni* ('nyee') *mo* (as in 'mom') *men* (as in 'men') *to* (as in 'dot')

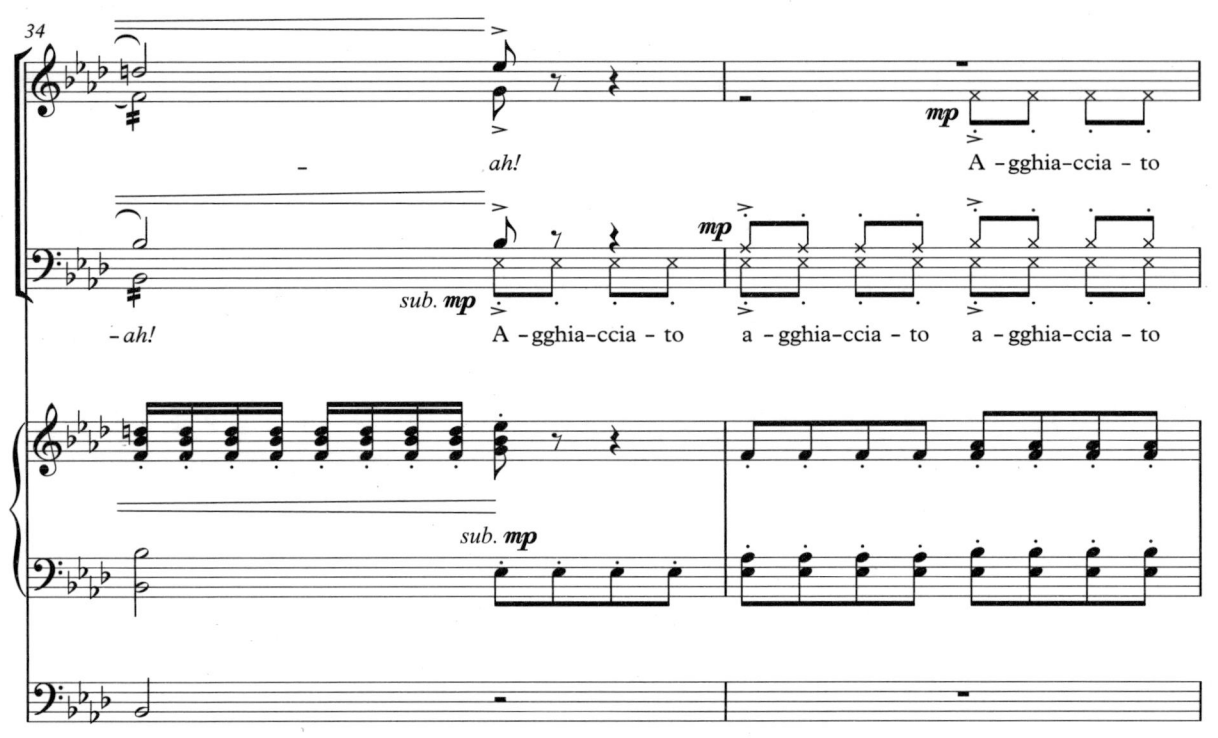
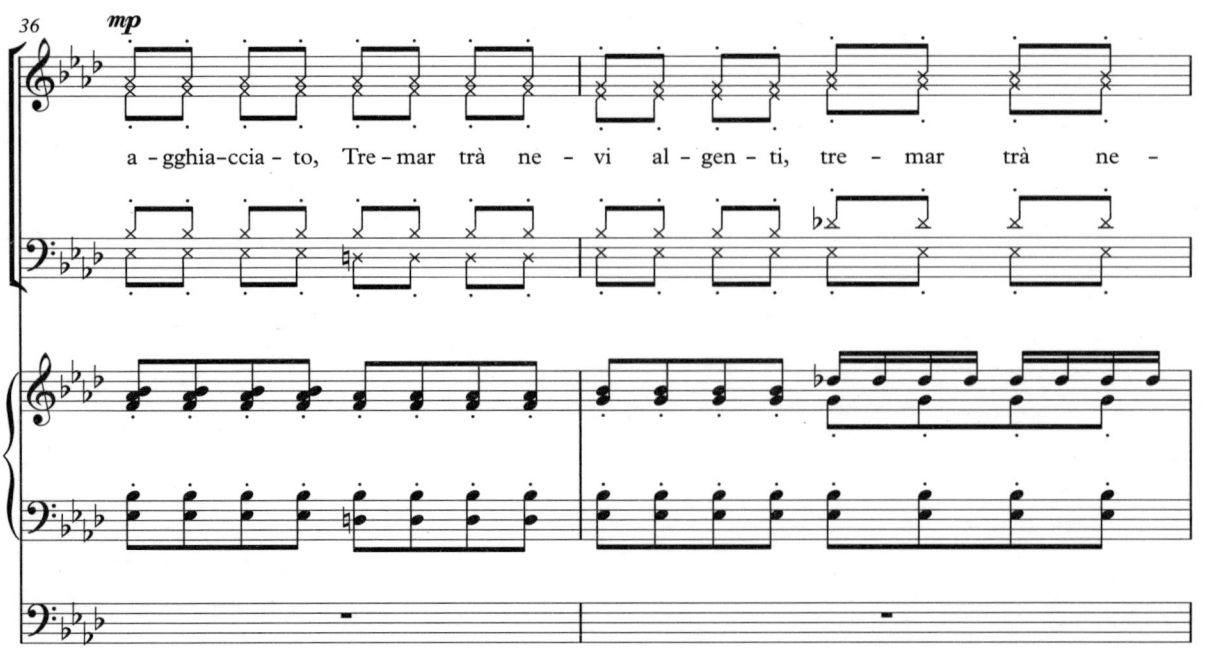

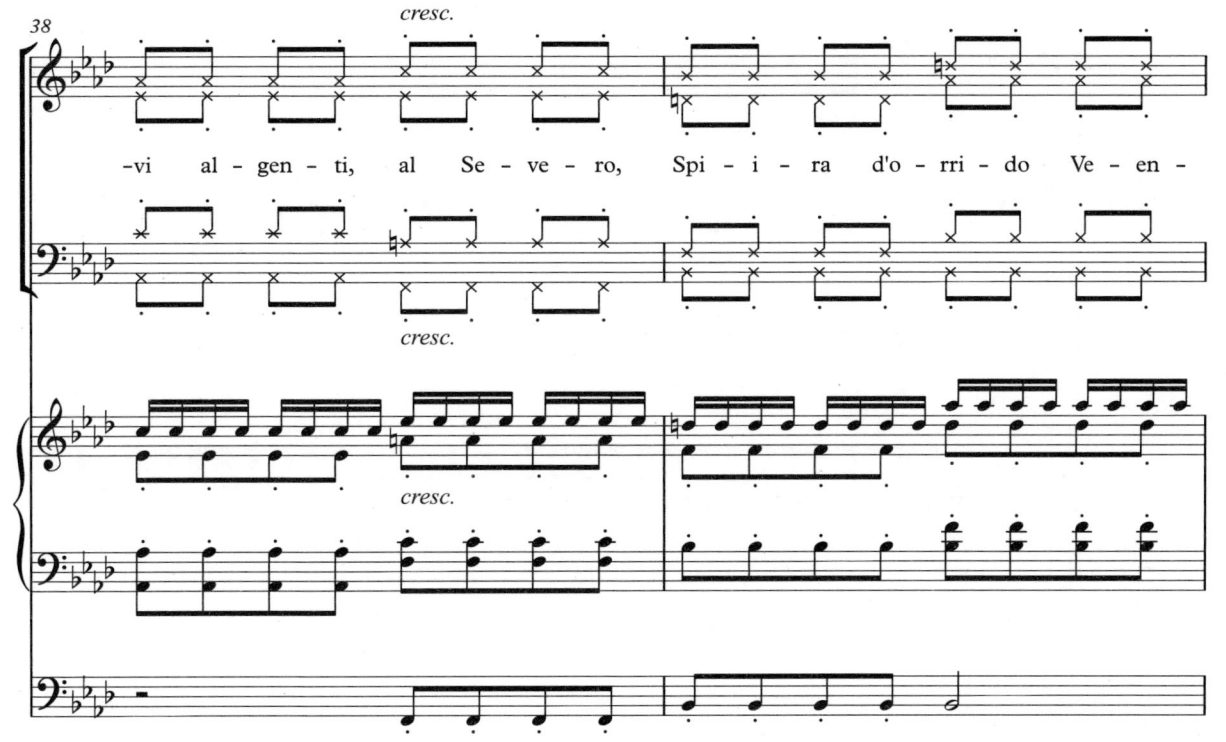

* Pronounced *e* (as in 'eh?') *pel* (as in 'belt') *So* (as in 'song') *ver* (as in 'very') *chio* ('kyo')
gel (as in 'jelly') *bat* (as in 'bat') *ter* (as in 'dare') *i* (as in 'eat') *den* (as in 'dentures') *ti* (as in 'deal')

-do! i pie-di og - ni mo - men - to.

Brrr!

In memory of Ward Swingle (1927–2015)

12. Cosy Indoors
(while outside it pours)

Scat syllables in the style of the
original 1960s Swingle Singers

Antonio Vivaldi arr.
Joanna Forbes L'Estrange

SATB choirs perform this movement *a cappella*. If strings are accompanying the other movements, the Bass line could be doubled by *pizzicato* cello / double bass.

Upper voice choirs perform all vocal lines except the Bass, which will be played by the organ or *pizzicato* cello / double bass.

88

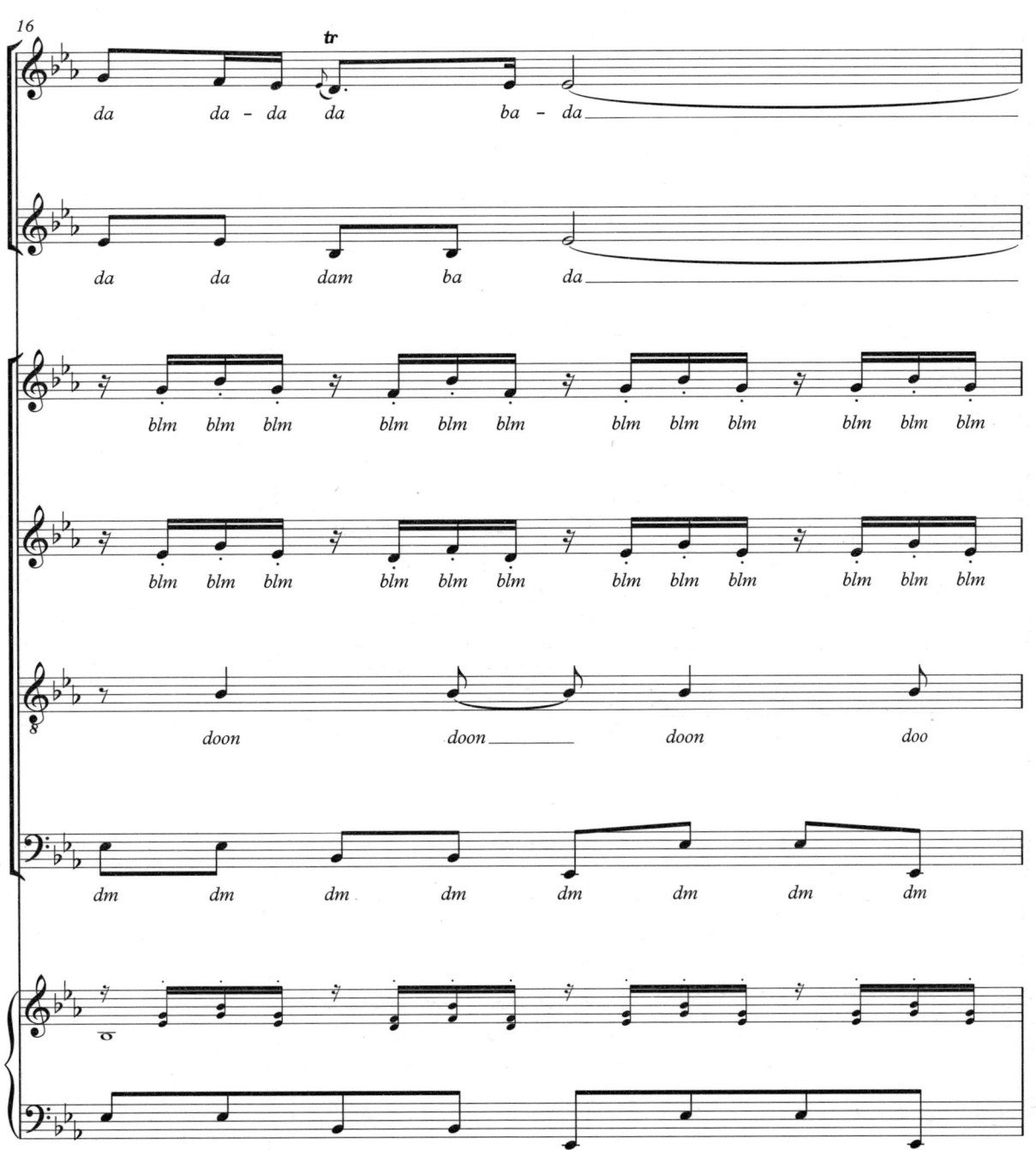

13. While Earth Remaineth

Genesis 8:22 (KJV)

Antonio Vivaldi arr.
Joanna Forbes L'Estrange

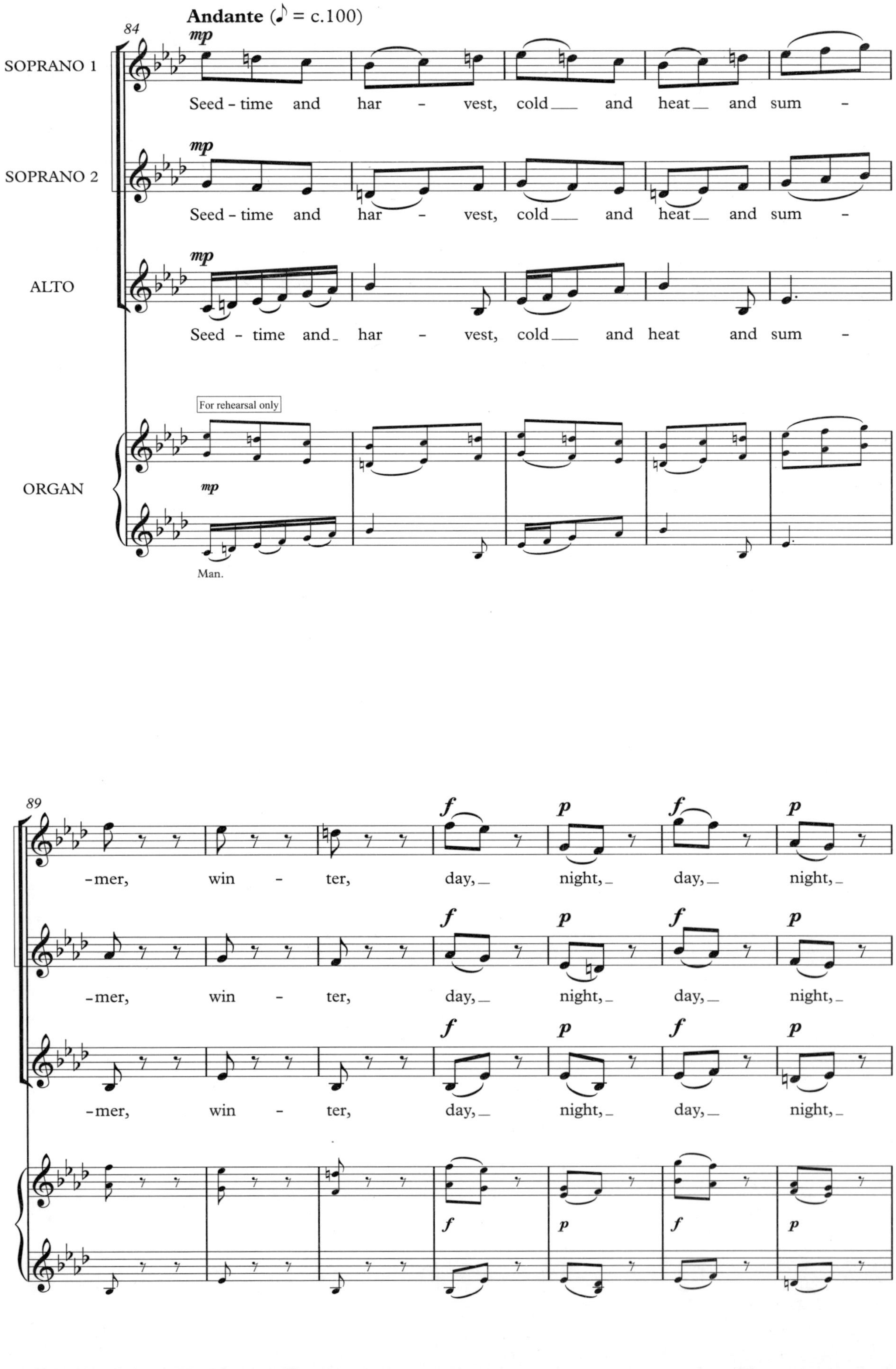
Andante (♪ = c.100)
84
SOPRANO 1
SOPRANO 2
ALTO
ORGAN
For rehearsal only
mp
Seed - time and har - vest, cold and heat and sum -
Seed - time and har - vest, cold and heat and sum -
Seed - time and har - vest, cold and heat and sum -
Man.
89
f
p
-mer, win - ter, day, night, day, night,
-mer, win - ter, day, night, day, night,
-mer, win - ter, day, night, day, night,

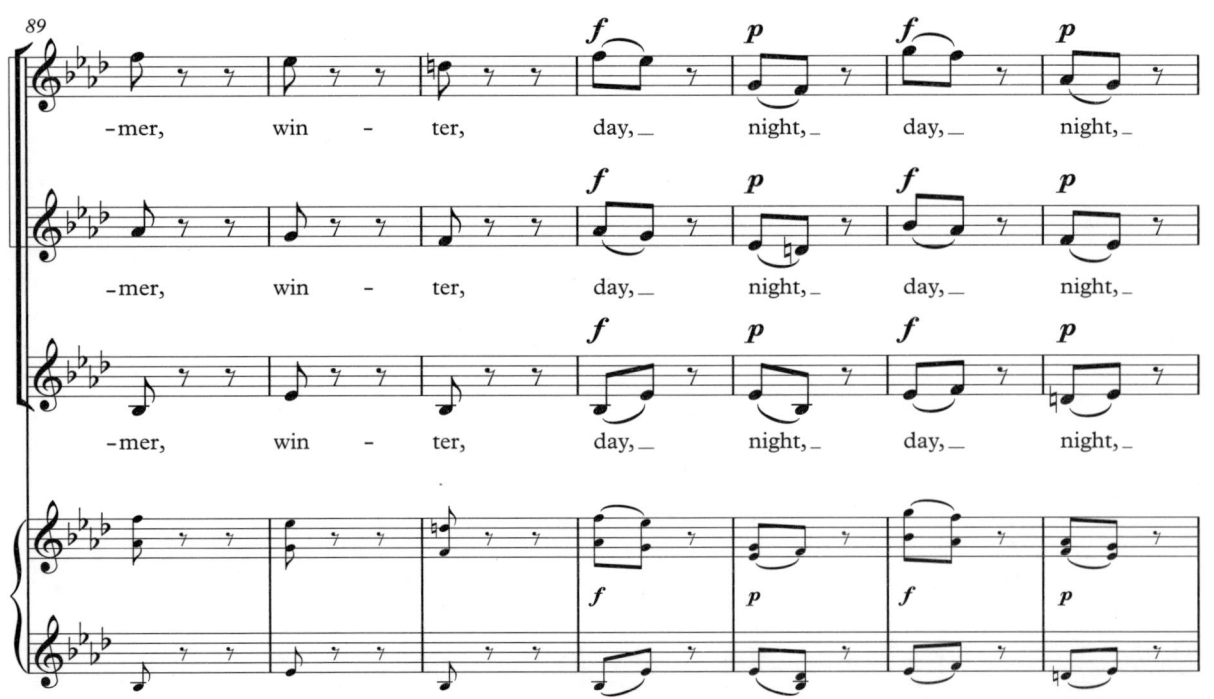

96
mf
all shall not cease, all shall not
mp
mf
all shall not cease, all shall not
mp
mf
all shall not cease, all shall not
mp
mf
mp

103
Più mosso (♪ = c.108)
cease.
cease.
cease.
f
Ped.

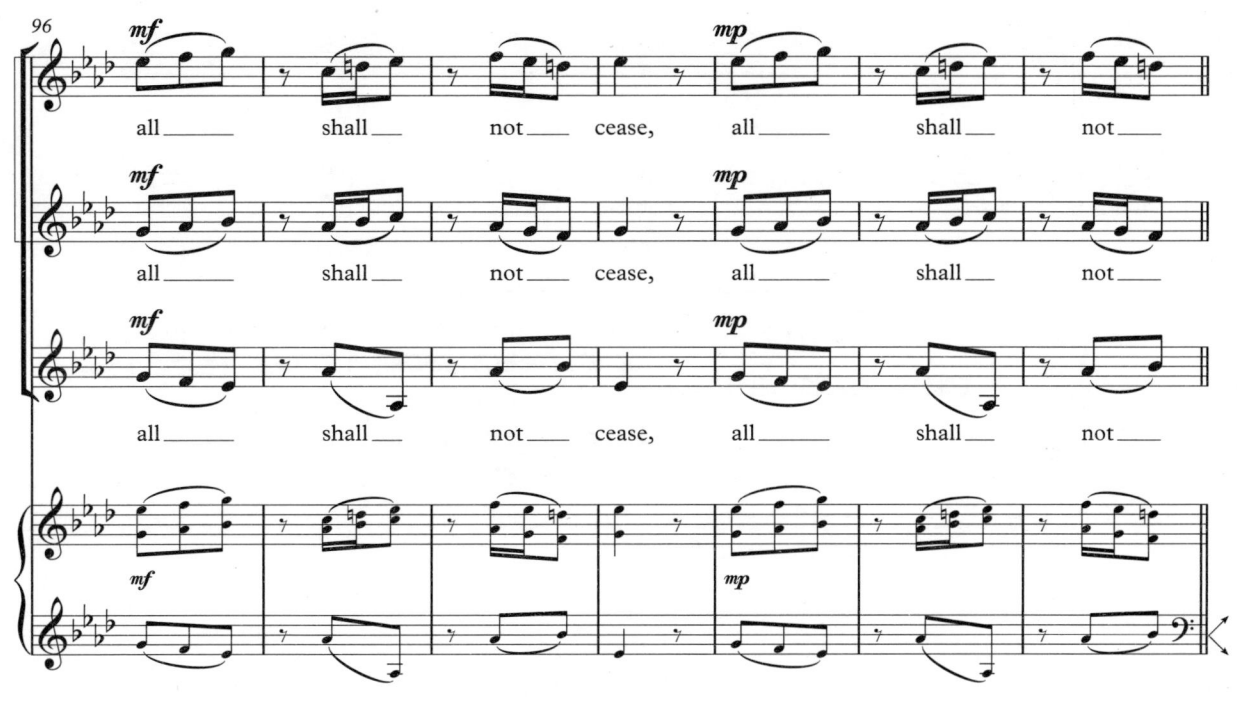

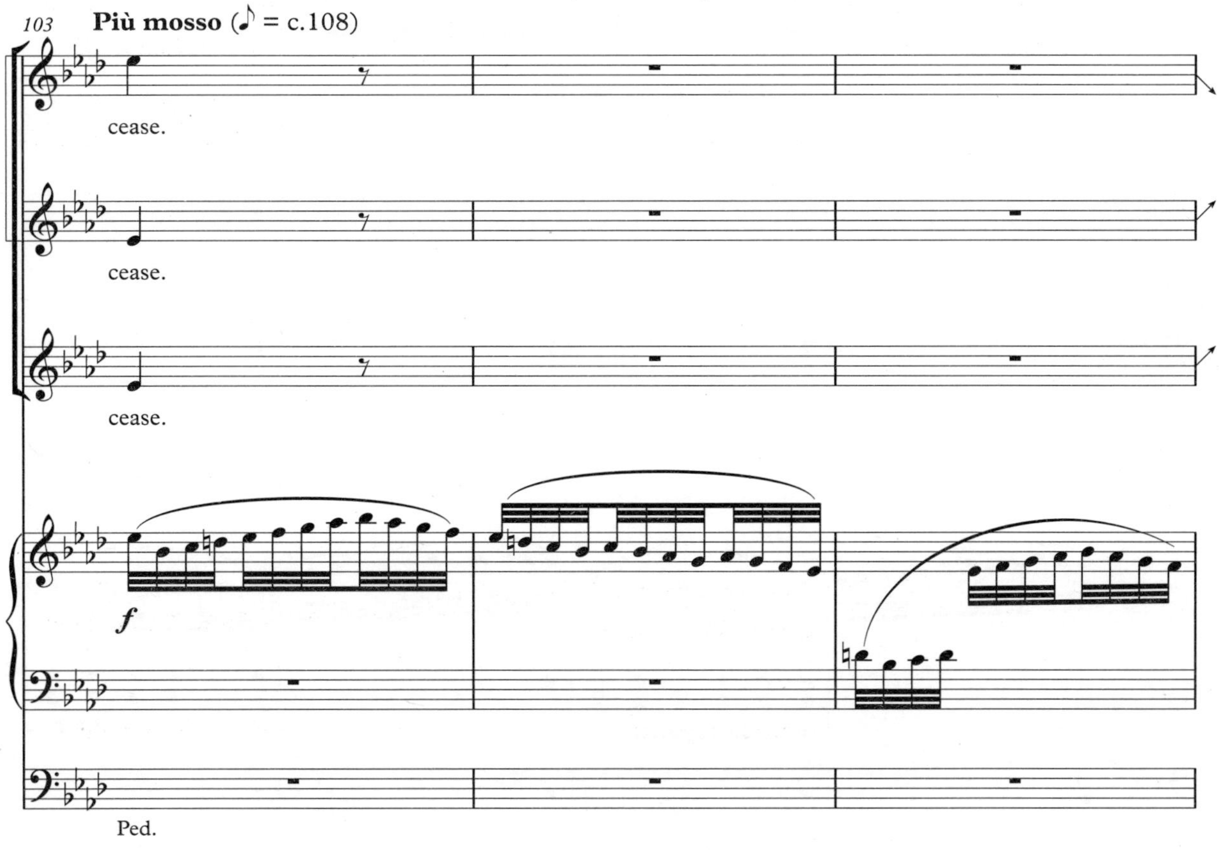

117
earth re – main – eth,
120
SOPRANO
ALTO
TENOR
BASS
ORGAN
f
SPRING,
Mu – sic, sweet mu – sic.
Mu – sic, sweet mu – sic.
SPRING,
Solo

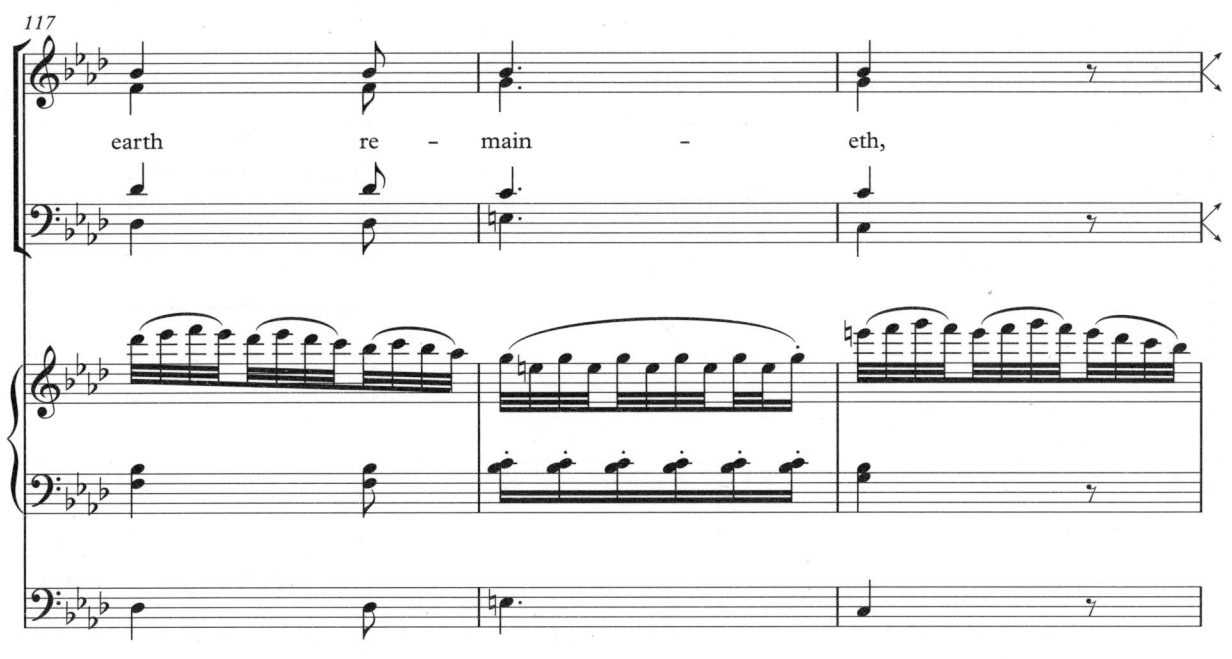

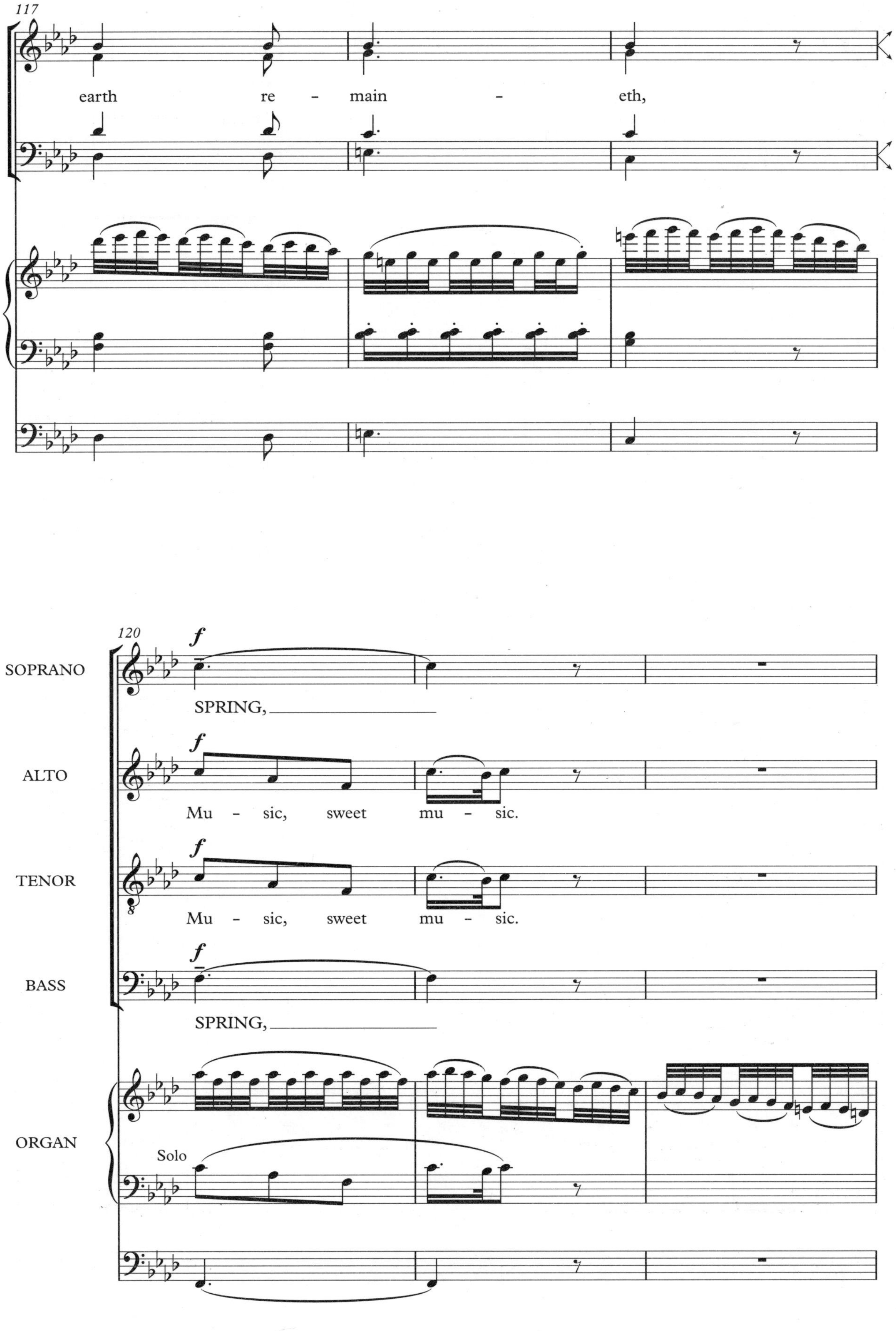

14. A Time of Peace

Ecclesiastes 3:1 & 5–8 (KJV)
Additional words by Joanna Forbes L'Estrange

Joanna Forbes L'Estrange

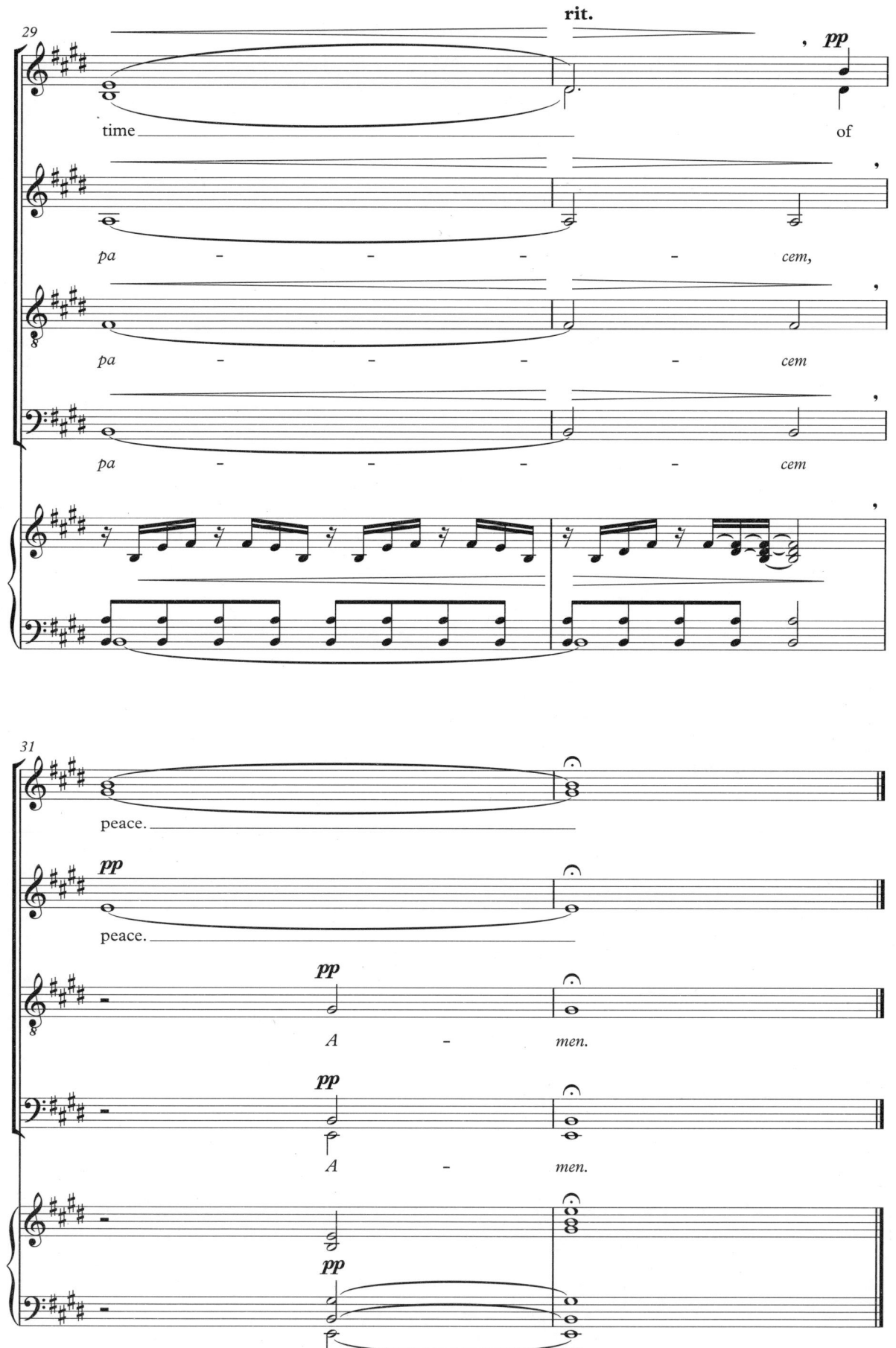

Performance notes

Scoring
The piece can be performed by SATB choirs and by upper voice choirs. Throughout the score, passages with small note-heads are for upper voice choirs only. Choirs have the option to perform *A Season to Sing* with organ OR with strings (vln I/vln II/vla/cello/d.bass) and keyboard continuo. There are also optional parts for flute x2, trumpet x2 and trombone x2. All instrumental parts can be hired from the RSCM.

Presentation
Choirs are encouraged to use their imagination when preparing concert performances of this work. Suggestions include coloured lighting which changes with each season, a group of folk dancers, seasonal images projected onto a screen above the performers, extra sound effects for thunder and lightning...

Programming
Although the composer's intention is that *A Season to Sing* be performed in its entirety - the approximate total duration is 40 minutes - it would be possible to perform any one of the seasons as a set of three pieces within the context of a mixed programme. For companion pieces, choir directors would do well to consider madrigals or part-songs on the theme of the seasons or nature. Alexander L'Estrange's three settings for SATB/piano, *Love's Philosophy*, would make an ideal pairing with *A Season to Sing*.

Movement by movement

1. A Time to Dance
This opening movement and its partner (mvt.14) are composed in a quasi-Baroque style to complement the Vivaldi. Attention to diction is important so that the words are clear for the audience. The final 'a time to dance' should be sung with energy and a smile, to set up the first movement of Spring.

2. Welcome Spring
Note that the tempo marking is slower than in Vivaldi's original concerto. Observing the Allegro leggiero will ensure that the 'fa-la-las' are light and madrigal-like. If your choir does not boast enough proficient whistlers, the birdsong chorus can be doubled by or performed by the organist or string players instead. Ideally, though, this section would be unaccompanied to draw maximum attention to the whistlers.

3. Music, Sweet Music

This movement is twice the length of Vivaldi's original to accommodate two of Eliza Cook's verses from her poem 'Spring' which so perfectly fit the style and subject matter.

4. To the Bagpipe's Sound

The effect of the accompanying bagpipe drone is achieved by creating a nasal tone on the 'air' syllable. As in movement 2, the 'fal-la-las' should be light and madrigal-like.

5. Sing Cuccu!

Choirs should aim for as much contrast as possible between the languid 'summer moonlight' sections, the energetic, cuckoo passage and the final run to find shelter from the imminent storm.

6. Trees Lending Shelter

In this rare opportunity to sing a whole movement in unison, aim for a perfect blend between voices. At the end of the movement, vocal scores will need to be placed on chairs/music stands/floor, leaving hands free for the body percussion of the next movement.

7. Summer Storm

Note that the voice parts are paired Soprano/Tenor and Alto/Bass in order to maximise the range of sounds within each part as well as to make the sounds appear from different places within the choir. Upper voice choirs will simply divide into Sopranos and Altos. This movement requires a dramatic delivery, both vocally and physically.

8. Song of Harvest

The beginning of Autumn presents SATB choirs with their first moment of unaccompanied singing. As with movement 2, in order to make the words intelligible, the opening tempo here is significantly slower than in the original violin concerto. For the slow section, a solo soprano from the choir should sing the higher notes while the rest of the soprano section remains on the tutti vocal line.

9. Falling Autumn Leaves

Emily Brontë's evocative words, coupled with Vivaldi's music, creates a vivid picture of lying under an autumn tree, watching the leaves as they fall gently to the ground.

10. Make a Joyful Noise

Vivaldi's programmatic depiction of a hunt has been re-imagined as a song of praise for a good harvest. What were hunting horns are now the sounding trumpets of Psalm 150.

11. Winter Freeze

The words for this movement are taken from the first part of Vivaldi's *L'Inverno* sonnet, which translates as:

> Shivering, frozen by icy snow
> And the fierce gusts of a horrible wind
> Running, stomping incessantly,
> Teeth chattering from the intense cold
>
> Translation by Jeremy Sadler

The individual syllables of the Italian, especially when half sung, half whispered, lend themselves perfectly to creating a wintery soundscape.

12. Cosy Indoors (while outside it pours)

The inspiration for this movement comes from the second part of Vivaldi's *L'Inverno* sonnet which describes being warm and cosy by the fire while it pours with rain outside. Arranged in the style of the original Swingle Singers, the *blm blm blm* part represents the raindrops while the melody lines evoke the fireside scene. Choirs should employ minimal or no vibrato for this movement, aiming for an 'instrumental' singing style in which accuracy of pitch and rhythm is paramount. For further guidance on how to achieve an authentic, Swingle sound it is suggested that choirs listen to the album *Jazz Sébastien Bach*.

13. While Earth Remaineth

Instead of the winter scene portrayed in Vivaldi's original, this choral version employs a Biblical text which neatly draws together the themes of the piece, providing a fitting conclusion to the four seasons.

14. A Time of Peace

As well as being the finale to the whole piece this movement is also the second half of movement 1, setting the remaining four lines from the same Ecclesiastes passage. The composer's insertion of the words 'no more' (b.23-24, immediately after 'a time of war') is in reference to the turbulent times during which *A Season to Sing* was published. The final words *A time of peace* are sung in conjunction with the *Dona nobis pacem* phrase from the Requiem mass.

A Season to Sing
was co-commissioned by the following choirs
in England, N. Ireland, Scotland, Wales, Jersey, Canada, USA, South Africa, Vietnam & Australia

Abbey Consort

Amici Cantate

Barts Academic Festival Choir & Orchestra

Botley Choral Society, Hampshire

The British International School of Ho Chi Minh City Choirs

The Castle Choir, Berkhamsted

Cheltenham Youth Choir

Choralia Milford Tony Hales' Legacy Fund

Clerkenwell Community Choir

The Combined Community Choirs of Rugby

Darlington Choral Society

Downing Place United Reformed Church Choir, Cambridge

Grace United Church Choir, Nova Scotia

Harpenden Choral Society

Hickory Neck Episcopal Church Choir

Holmchase Singers

The King's Counterpoint

MidLife ChoirSis

Ross Penyard Singers

Sounds Connected Community Chorus

St Mark with St Margaret, Plumstead Common

St Paul's Episcopal Cathedral Choir, Dundee

The Choir of Trinity College, Melbourne

TRUE VOICES, South Africa

Victoria Park Singers

Walton Voices

Wigton Choral Society

The Yorkshire Decibelles

Alyth Choral Society

Alresford Community Choir

Blundell's Senior School Choir

The Boundstone Chorus

Cantemus Chamber Choir, Wales

The Cecilia Consort

The Choirs of the Cathedral of St. John, Albuquerque

Classical Chorus, Hertfordshire

Codetta Choirs

Croxley Green Community Choir

Dartford Choral Society

Finsbury Park Singers

Guildford Chamber Choir

Harrow Choral Society

Highgate Choral Society

Kendal South Choir

LUMINOSA

Pontefract Choral Society

Selly Park Singers, Birmingham

St Dunstan's Church Choir, Mayfield

St Mary's, Balcombe, West Sussex

Sydney Philharmonia Choirs

Trinity Evangelical Lutheran Church, Laramie

Tyndale Choral Society

Voce Chamber Choir

Wareham Choral Society

Worthing Choral Society

A time of war no more
Dona nobis pacem

More choral pieces by Joanna Forbes L'Estrange published by RSCM publications

Anthems

Drop, drop, slow tears

Faith, hope and love

God the Holy Trinity

Go forth in peace

How can I keep from singing?

Let my prayer rise up

The mountains shall bring peace - The RSCM Coronation Anthem

Saint Richard's Prayer

The Chorister's Prayer

The Lord's Prayer

Words from the Cross

Carols

Advent 'O' Carol

Carol of the Crib

I will hold Him

In the bleak midwinter

Jesus Christ is born today

Love came down

Song of the shepherds

Winter Light

Music for the Liturgy

King's College Service - Magnificat and Nunc Dimittis

Preces and Responses

Psalm 135

The St Helen's Service - Communion service